IN THE
MIDST
OF THE
STORMS

A Story of Trauma, Faith, and Hope

JON SADLER

In the Midst of the Storms: A Story of Trauma, Faith, and Hope

http://www.jonsadlerbooks.com

For more information contact:

BRIMINGSTONE PRESS

WWW.BRIMINGSTONE.PRESS

5301 Alpha Rd, Suite 80 #200
Dallas, TX 75254

Book and Cover design by *Brimingstone Press*

ISBN: 978-1-953562-00-5

For the caregivers who provide the lifeline needed to survive the storms

Contents

Preface

All the characters, locations, and events in this story were formulated through years of experience in helping people struggling with the unknowns of epilepsy or stroke and the stress those who cared for them experienced. The people who responded often needed as much support as the person with the seizures and, without consideration for themselves, provided the first aid necessary for their loved one. Young children of a parent with a chronic illness can mature at a very early age. The parts of this story which describe a stroke, seizure, treatment, and the subsequent recovery are accurate.

To better understand the trauma that occurs it is important to understand that people with epilepsy have been mistreated for thousands of years. Alleged as cases of demon possession, they were treated with separation and exorcism up to today. Isolation and sterilization were standard until 1950. Laws banning marriage for epileptics were in place through 1980, and the Americans with Disabilities Act had to be revised to appropriately address people with epilepsy in 2008. Discrimination continues to occur today, no matter the gender or race.

Ironically, recent studies have found that many people with epilepsy experience a closeness with God that only a few people ever experience. Much of this occurs through visions or voices heard during the ictal or post ictal stages of a seizure, a time when all the defenses of the mind are incapacitated. This may explain the voices and visions that occurred to many people in the Bible, and others with key roles in various religions. The Romans and Greeks thought epilepsy to be a sacred disease.

This is a story based on how people worked through the physical and mental challenges brain injury creates and their ability to survive through faith when they could not understand everything that was happening around them. Recovery is possible even when the part of the brain that controls the emotions of sadness, despair, and fear blocks the ability to reason and understand the outcome.

My hope is that this story can reach out to those of you who are struggling with an incident that is burned into your memory or who are providing care in situations where dealing with trauma is often a part of your work—be it to a friend, a family member, as an emergency responder, or as someone working in the medical field. May this help you find a sense of peace and a clearer understanding of your role.

Storms

They expressed God's love as their calling
In ways thought best deserved
To share the Word that Christ had brought
Through the ministries they served

The seizures came like massive storms
Driving dread deep in their souls
She suffered with the onslaught
As her memory the struggle stole

The storms raged through both their minds
The present and the past
The day would come when the seizures won
And hope was lost at last

His heart was torn, where was God?
The response his emotions buried
But love could never be destroyed
In their souls the answer's carried

Section I

The Storms

The traumatic events have past, but unlike a physical injury, recovery never ends. The scars exist but are not visible. Sharing the experience was another step towards helping me find meaning to what happened.

It was a bright and warm Monday morning, the first day of a weeklong seminar about living with stress. My part in it was to give a presentation about living with the stress of a chronic disease. The group was diverse and consisted of patients and their families, hospital staff and doctors, pastors, priests, and graduate students studying to be counselors. They all had a desire to learn about helping people who suffered from traumatic experiences while caring for a person with a chronic condition. It seemed like a great opportunity to share my life experience, especially on a subject not covered well in text or in a classroom.

Carol, the administrator of the seminar, was about to introduce me. With a PhD in counseling, her focus was on helping people living with trauma, several of whom were in the audience. We were in a research facility, and the staff took care of many difficult cases which left lasting impressions, some were resolved with miracles through healing but many brought distress because the treatment failed. She gave me a smile and said, "If you are ready, I will introduce you." I nodded, and she walked over to the center of the floor.

The room went quiet as she came up to the podium. I sensed everyone knew who she was as she welcomed them to the seminar. She then introduced me by saying, "Mr. Johnson has a degree in counseling and will be sharing his experience and providing insight about the type of trauma all of you may experience. He will share how stress in people who are caring for someone on a continual basis can build and become overwhelming, what may happen, and how to help. Let us welcome Mr. Johnson." There was an applause, and Carol gave me her big smile and shook my hand before sitting down in front.

As I looked out over the auditorium, I started with "They say the best way to treat post-traumatic stress disorder [PTSD] is to replay the situation over and over. For those who are responsible for the care for others, this may not be effective as the situation being experienced repeats itself. We know that emotions are controlled through reasoning. When they dominate the mind, we can no longer comprehend what is actually happening, and control of oneself is often lost. Fear, depression, anxiety, and grief take over. Then what do you do? I have been on many sides of the spectrum—the patient, the mentor and counselor, and the caregiver. Sharing my experience in the past has been educational for people like you, but this time, it is also part of my recovery from loss. Everything I share with you this week really did happen."

The room lights dimmed. It was time to get into the details.

Chapter 1

My seizures started in 1963 when I was four years old. My sister Katie found me in bed early in the morning when she came in to tease me about her being up before me and then realized something was wrong. I was nonresponsive with an odd expression on my face. She tried to be the eight-year-old nurse and took my temperature. I bit the thermometer in two; fortunately, the mercury flowed out of my mouth. She became terrified and ran out of the room screaming. When our mother returned from the grocery store, she saw Katie downstairs crying and telling her, "Something is wrong with Matt." Our mom then shouted for me as she ran up the stairs. She saw me staring into empty space with part of my body convulsing and grabbed me from the bed to carry me as carefully as she could as she ran out to her car. She drove very fast, straight through stop signs and traffic lights as she sped to the hospital. Now my body had become completely rigid, and every muscle so tight it shook violently. I was slowly turning blue as my lungs could not fully function. She thought she was watching me, her youngest child, die.

In the emergency room the doctors immediately gave me oxygen, the shallowness of my breath limited its effectiveness. For more than eight hours, my body suffered from the electrical storm that was surging in my brain. As the storm continued, my parents were told there would probably be significant brain damage in the aftermath, and no one knew what I would be like once I woke up. As the hours passed, my mother and father sat beside me, and my siblings were at home dazed and terrified, not knowing what was happening to their brother. Finally, the seizure ended and with my body exhausted, I slept for many hours.

As I began to stir and my eyes opened, I saw my mother staring at me with an expression I'd never seen before. Her eyes were wet, and vivid lines running throughout her face which was white as snow. I remember wondering why she looked at me so intensely with such a worried and stressed expression. My stomach growled, and I felt hungry. So, I looked at her and said, "Mommy, I'm hungry." Her expression changed immediately, and she jumped from the chair as if I surprised her. "He's hungry! He's hungry!" she exclaimed. I had no idea why she was so excited. Once I had come back to life, her color returned, and she had a beaming smile. Little did anyone know that the torment was not over; the hell we would live with had just begun.

Within a few weeks, I was taken for testing to another hospital that specialized in treating people with epilepsy. I was to have an electroencephalogram, or EEG. This involved having many wires attached to my head, then being told to sleep as my mother and the technician walked out of the room. I was terrified because my mother was leaving me again like she had to when she took me to the hospital for the seizure. In those days, there were set visiting hours, and unless you were dying, no member of the family could stay with you overnight. I began to cry, and mother came running back into the room and held me, then she explained why she had to leave. She assured me she would be watching me, that she loved me, and would be taking me home soon. Her motherly love brought me peace, and the knowledge she was near allowed me to lie down and close my eyes. But I could not sleep, fearing something dreadful was going to happen, and it did.

When she came back into the room with the technician, she was not smiling like her usual self and had the worried look I saw when I woke up from the first seizure; the paleness and vivid lines on her face were back. The technician had shown her the results of the EEG, which showed that an electrical storm was occurring in a section of the left side of my brain. Although I only had the one seizure, the EEG indicated I would have more without treatment, and I was diagnosed as epileptic.

My parents would soon learn how very misunderstood epilepsy as a condition, really was. A close friend and our family doctor explained that a person struggling with seizures is often labeled and treated as mentally ill or unstable. At the time, several states had laws that prohibited people with epilepsy from getting married or going to school. In many cases, an epileptic child was placed in a special education group with children with learning disabilities. There were few known medications available for treatment, and the side effects of which could potentially be devastating. The lack of knowledge about epilepsy and the social stigma of the time influenced my mother's response to my diagnosis.

There were only three medications for treating epilepsy at the time, and the one selected for me was phenobarbital. The intention was to slow my brain down, calming the storm that was occurring in a section of it. Unfortunately, it slowed my whole brain down, including the sections processing all my cognitive abilities. When I was asked a question, I seemed to be unresponsive. The question had to be repeated several times before I was able to provide an answer. My rate of speech had slowed significantly, and my ability to laugh was nearly gone. The medication affected my bones, causing my teeth to darken. My siblings referred to me as the little old man because I behaved like someone who was very, very old.

My family witnessed a profound change as their energetic little boy, who had previously laughed and cried and done silly things as young children do, was no longer the same. I talked slower than the typical child, and my rate of speech would be impacted throughout my life by this first round of medication. Fortunately, I was on phenobarbital for only four years. I had that first seizure and was seizure-free while on the medication, so the doctors determined that an anticonvulsant was no longer needed.

Or so they thought. It would not be until many years later that it would be known through research that my experiences of *déjà vu*, and visions of "bugs" in the house were actually focal onset seizures with nonmotor symptoms. Maybe this was a good thing because dealing with this form of seizure was much easier than suffering with the side effects of the antiseizure drugs.[*]

---

[*] Since 1963, over thirty new medications have been developed and are used in the treatment of seizure disorders. However, personality changes, anger, severe depression, and memory loss are often caused by medication. Finding the right medication that works best includes evaluating the side effects and not just controlling the seizures. Doctors need to be made aware of any side effects, especially when the patient may not be able to realize what is happening.

Chapter 2

My brain was able to function normally again when I came off the medication. The delay the medication caused to my ability to process thoughts and respond to people and events was removed. I felt free and looked forward to a brighter future. For the next eight years, I was a fun-loving teenager living a full life. I had many friends, went on high-adventure camping trips, did very well in school, and was active in the community and church. I loved to repair things, like bicycles and all types of engines, and I even overhauled a car while in high school. Sailing was my joy because it required continual adjustments based on what could and couldn't be seen—such as the water and the wind. It was a form of training that prepared me to deal with the unknowns and fears that seizures brought into my life. When I turned eighteen, I determined it was time to earn a degree in engineering with the hope to someday work for the military. Another near-death experience came a year later that would impact the rest of my life.

The career opportunity came through acceptance to a state university with an excellent engineering program and a nationally rated sailing team. It was time to start studying to be an engineer with the excitement of meeting new people and joining the team. I crewed with a fellow sailor named Brian who was striving to achieve the all-American level in the competition ratings for sailboat racing.

The team did so well we were able to participate in the regional championship, where a sailing accident lead to a severe blow to my head and more damage to my brain.

The wind was blowing more than twenty knots and it was downright frigid. It was so cold, in fact, that we had to deal with snow squalls. We wore long-sleeved shirts and blue jeans and were covered with foul-weather gear and thin gloves to allow for gripping and releasing the lines, a thick wool-knit hat kept my head warm. When we got into the boats, we were cold. Yet with the high wind, we had to work hard and were quickly sweating. We didn't have to work so hard coming back to the dock after a race, except that within minutes we were freezing as the chilly wind blew through our clothing. We quickly slipped into parkas to stay warm as we watched our teammates sail their division.

The high wind was causing more and more damage to the boats, and people were losing control and flipping over. We realized the rigging was damaged in the last boat we got in, with the back of the boom hanging lower. We did not bother to try to repair it as there was not enough time before our race started. We figured we would make do.

There came a point where we needed to jibe to change course, a difficult maneuver in high winds. With the boom coming low in the boat now, it would come snapping across with tremendous power as we made the turn. We looked at each other with a moment of fear written on our faces, then Brian pulled the helm over. As he leaned back to get out of the way of the boom, he fell off the boat. His hand was so cold he could not let go of the tiller, and it broke off. I laid down in the boat, but as the boom came around, it slammed into the left side of my head, bounced up, and hit the water, causing the boat to topple over. I was thrown into the rigging. Within seconds, the boat was completely upside down.

It took several minutes for me to regain consciousness, and once I did, I was not able to move. Some lines were tangled around my legs, and Brian was pulling on the back of my foul-weather gear. He yanked so hard to get me out of the rigging it tore off one of the legs of my gear. Once clear, he pulled me around to the back of the boat. "Grab onto the rudder mount!" he yelled. But I could not hear him. Everything was in slow motion. The waves kept bashing us into the back of the boat, and he could not hang on.

I wanted to say something, but the words were just not there. Eventually, my ability to hear and grasp what was happening returned. Brian was holding on to me and the hull of the boat as best he could. Once he realized I could comprehend what he said and react appropriately, he got us on opposite sides so we could straddle the bottom while holding onto each other.

We wondered if we would be rescued in time. We were freezing and drifted very close to a huge suspension bridge. As we waited for help, I saw my wool hat floating away. I hadn't realized at the time how the thickness of the wool had cushioned the blow to my head, saving my life. We were washed off the boat hull several times by a wave. Then as the boat came down into the swell of another wave, we grabbed hold of each other and were lifted partly out of the water as the boat was brought to the top of the next wave. We were tired and extremely cold, we struggled to hang on.

Eventually, a rescue boat arrived and picked us up. Recovering the boat was not a priority as the pilot saw we needed immediate medical attention. By the time we reached the boathouse, my whole body was blue and shaking uncontrollably from the cold. The staff immediately took me into the locker room and got me into a shower, drenching me with warm water for more than thirty minutes, trying to get my body temperature back to normal. My head hurt terribly and throbbed where the boom had hit it. No one realized at the time, however, the extent of the damage to my brain.

Eventually, the boat was recovered and brought back to the boathouse. It was completely destroyed. The hull was cracked from one end to the other, the rigging was broken, the jib was ripped in two, and the mainsail was torn. The boom was badly dented and warped where it had hit my head. The rudder was never found.

There was a huge knot swelling on the left side of my head. The coach looked me over and asked if I would be okay for the two-hour ride back to the campus. I assured him everything would be fine. We climbed into the car, and I fell fast asleep from the exhaustion of the day. Years later, we would learn about concussions and the importance of seeking medical attention and to not let a person sleep while monitoring for internal bleeding. Not seeking such medical attention in my case had dire consequences.

I didn't realize the extent of the damage to my brain until the day after the accident. I took a history exam which involved writing essays and providing the details of historical events. I could provide most of the facts but could not complete the paragraphs and sentences. Within a week, I was having odd nauseous feelings, and my hands would shake for several minutes. Thirty years later, it would be discovered that these were focal onset aware seizures.

Chapter 3

The grand mal seizures began a year after the sailing accident. I had been studying for an exam and felt extremely anxious, so anxious that I couldn't sleep. Eating breakfast and lunch was difficult. I felt like vomiting once I put food in my mouth. My hand shook so much the soup spilled out of the spoon before it got to my mouth.

I was given the exam in an auditorium with more than three hundred students. I astonished my classmates by screaming, and they watched as I stood up and fell between the rows of seats and students. Those near me were shocked as I vomited, and my body went stiff and shook uncontrollably.

My tongue was clenched between my teeth, and blood flowed out of my mouth. A fellow student stepped in to help as he knew what to do because his father had seizures too. Someone called the paramedics, and within minutes, I was rushed to the infirmary.

The first thing I wanted to do after regaining consciousness was to complete the exam. The storm that had been going on in my brain had left, and the equations I needed to solve the exam problems returned to my mind. The doctor called the professor to update him of my condition, then he told me the professor was waiting to see me once I was discharged. Since the doctor understood my history with seizures and because this was my first grand mal seizure in fifteen years, he changed his treatment plan. He didn't allow me to leave and called my mother to inform her of my seizure and his recommendation for me to obtain appropriate medical treatment. I would be monitored at the infirmary until my mother or father arrived.

My mother then called my father, who worked nearer the campus. He was always calm and one of the last to leave the building on a normal basis. However, this was the first time his staff had seen him quickly run out of the building early as he told an associate that his son had a seizure. He set a speed record driving to the campus. Meanwhile, I was totally exhausted and had slept until he arrived.

My dad smiled at me as he walked into the examination room and the doctor told him the details of the seizure and the care they provided. He was relieved to see I was able to talk and stand on my own as he had vivid memories of my first seizure and remembered that it lasted for hours. I was still wearing the shirt I had covered in vomit, so instead of heading home, we walked to my dormitory room where I could shower and change clothes.

The following week, I saw a neurologist and was told the seizure was a freak accident, however, he still put me on an anticonvulsant medication. There was much I needed to catch-up on after missing a week of classes, including taking a make-up exam for the one I could not complete. This time I had no issues with seizures, or my memory and I did very well.

Three weeks after seeing the neurologist, the state suspended my driver's license for a year. This brought me into a state of severe depression, caused in part by having to sell the car I refurbished, but also because I had to rely on others for rides. Six months after that, came another seizure in a classroom that scared many people, including myself. My diagnosis was changed from seizure disorder to epilepsy, and they reset the clock on my license suspension. Several students whom I once considered friends would no longer associate with me. My father told me, "Never tell anyone you have epilepsy!" He knew of the state laws forbidding marriage of people with epilepsy and was concerned about me being labelled and not allowed to live a normal life. The potential stigma was implanted in my mine and I believed lying about my condition was necessary in order to survive. But it was a secret that could not always be kept as I never had total control of the seizures. The fear of a seizure occurring became normal for me and my family to live with.

Medication did not stop my seizures; it simply prevented them from spreading to other sections of the brain that would disable my cognitive skills and cause the muscles throughout my body to seize. An aura would come with a wave of nausea and rapid heartbeat, then stop after a few minutes.[*] The auras and medication affected my memory, making it difficult for me to answer fill-in-the-blank type of questions. However, my ability to do math and engineering skills were not affected. Medication caused me to speak slower than normal, and several of my classmates thought my IQ was low but were impressed with my leadership or motivation skills in completing team projects and that I was in the top of the engineering class.

Being able to accomplish the work I needed to do did not stop the depression and suicidal ideations that came along, however. Even though my grades and social life seemed to be doing well, the impact seizures had on my driving and the inability to be independent led to days of depression, and a few times brought on suicidal ideations, such as thoughts that life wasn't worth living. It would not be until years later that research revealed that some or all such thoughts were brought about by the seizure medication. It would have made things easier to have known this at the time, but knowledge of this became a life saver several years later.

I graduated on time, after four years of college. A job offer then came from the US Navy in a place 800 miles from my school. Even with the setbacks I had with seizures, they seemed under control, my license had been reinstated and my dreams of working for the Navy were coming true. At that time, it was impossible to comprehend how the challenges of living with epilepsy would be

---

[*] An aura occurs in the preictal (beginning) stage of a seizure. It may be a premonition or may involve feelings such as déjà vu, impending doom, fear, nausea, or euphoria. Visual changes, hearing abnormalities, or changes in the sense of smell can also be auras. See appendix B for description and more details.

magnified by public misconceptions and the associated stigmas they create.

Chapter 4

It seemed impossible that I would be working for the US Navy, but it was now happening. The first day I was required to undergo an extensive physical so the government could be sure employees did not have a condition that they could later claim was the result of exposure to the elements in the shipyard or stress associated with working at the naval base. The doctor seemed bored, like this was just another case to sign off on. He even slouched over his desk as he reviewed the physical and blood tests completed that day. Suddenly he stood very straight and said, "Lookie here, I've got me a goddamn freak. The only thing you'll be allowed to do is sharpen pencils." I was crushed. I walked out and nearly quit, but then became determined to prove him wrong.

My supervisor was completely opposite to the doctor. He introduced me to Mark, another of his employees who also had epilepsy. Within a few weeks Mark and I became best friends like we had known each other for years. We enjoyed boating, water skiing, sailing, fishing, and shrimping. Fixing cars and repairing furniture were our hobbies. We supported each other by eating well, getting plenty of sleep, and playing hard. Eventually we both owned small boats and lived on a barrier island near the intracoastal waterway, but the most important part was that we were each other's support in controlling our fears of epilepsy. Even though a seizure killed him twenty-five years later, his story set an example in the life he lived, accomplishing more than most people while facing his fears.

I was then transferred to the construction division, another section of the Navy, and became a construction manager. This was during the height of the Cold War, and the waterfront and piers I was assigned to were neglected and in terrible condition. The

President was increasing the size of the Navy from 350 to 800 ships, and it was critical to have the piers fully operational to support some of them. The high level of responsibility given to me made me excited and anxious. I was excited to be overseeing the renovation of the waterfront facilities involving the upgrades and construction of piers, critical to ship operations, and anxious that my brain would falter, and a seizure would break-through.

What helped me in overcoming the dread of having a seizure was that I was in my twenties and had limited experience and knowledge of the seizures. With effective medications and me not realizing that the weird feelings of anxiety and rapid heartbeat was a seizure, I felt invincible. I had had my wisdom teeth removed and, within a couple of weeks, I thought of going windsurfing, which is essentially standing on a surfboard with a sail attached. It was a perfect day with the way the wind was blowing and the ocean waves being manageable. My parents were visiting and stayed on the beach and watched. An aura started when I was about a half mile from shore.

I had hoped that this was just an aura and my medication would make it go away, but this time, it continued to progress and spread throughout most of my brain, becoming a complex partial seizure. I lost control of my body and let go of the sail. My ability to reason was gone and it seemed best to walk away, so I stepped off into the water. With no life jacket on, my body continued to sink deeper and deeper, and the light got dimmer. Typically, seizures would cause me to lose total consciousness, but this time I was standing behind the portal of my eye, watching my arms float out in front of me, nonresponsive and feeling like they were not a part of me—just objects floating in the water. The fear and dread caused by a seizure had disappeared, leaving me in total peace, surrounded by a presence that made me feel safe and free. My eye was like a window my body was standing behind, watching in awe as I drifted down into the chasm of the ocean. That was when I heard a voice say, "Not yet, Matt. I have plans for you."

Suddenly, I became conscious of the real world again. My awareness returned and it registered in my mind that my body was under water, sinking rapidly. Control of my arms and legs returned immediately, and I was able to swim quickly toward the surface. I needed to breathe, but knew if this happened, it would cause my death. It seemed to take forever to reach the surface. Eventually, my lungs won out and began to exhale, and I broke the surface just before inhaling. The voice I heard was correct. I would make it back, but I was confused and totally exhausted. Seizures often left me with little energy, and my body burned even more with the adrenaline rush involved in reaching the surface. The windsurfer was gone, and the beach was too far away to swim with what little energy was left. Panic began to set in as I jerked my head to look around me. The bow of the windsurfer appeared, then was gone; it was less than a foot away behind me. My lack of peripheral vision kept me from seeing it sooner. It would take a while for me to reset from the seizure.

Even climbing onto the board took energy, which I struggled to find. I laid on the board for quite a while before standing up. The sail felt like it weighed hundreds of pounds as I pulled it out of the water. Sailing was exceedingly difficult, but eventually I reached the beach and when I attempted to step off the board, I fell into the shallow water. The board washed up onto the beach as I crawled out and collapsed. My mother and a fellow engineer were soon with me; mother immediately knew what had happened and what to do. I managed to walk home, changed my clothes, and collapsed on my bed for several hours. It would take days for me to fully recover.

Those who witnessed what happened, along with my parents, were given only minimal details. My father had taught me to just live with it. I learned to take the rules my second neurologist gave me seriously: eat well, stay hydrated, maintain low levels of mental stress, respect my body, no alcohol, and take my medication as directed. When sick or injured, I had to give myself plenty of time to heal. I prayed and made a contract with God because I knew there was no one else who could cure me. It was a simple contract: "Please give me twenty years of control of the seizures, and I will be a good man." Everything worked well for several years as the seizures were controlled as I followed the medical rules.

Eventually, I met the love of my life, Becky. Our love for each other blossomed, and we were married a year after we met. It felt like heaven to have work, marriage, and friends. My doctor looked at my history and finding I hadn't had a grand mal seizure for several years, decided to take me off the medication. I was excited at first to be free of it, and with my contract with the Lord, I had no worries. However, a couple of weeks later, I started feeling nervous all the time, triggered by the smallest of things, like the thought of eating without spilling my food, with moments of extreme feelings of anxiety. Within two weeks, a grand mal seizure happened at home, right in front of Becky. She was terrified as she watched my body jerking on the floor, slowly turning blue from not being able to breathe, and seeing blood trickling out of my mouth as I chewed on my tongue. She ran to the phone to call 911 and waited for the ambulance to arrive.

I had felt the seizure coming as my level of anxiety increased for several hours, and that was when a wave of nausea raced through my body. My awareness returned when I felt my shirt being ripped open by the paramedics. The seizure storm in my brain disabled my other senses, causing me to be blind and deaf. Eventually, I could begin to hear voices, and my vision partially returned. The paramedics were asking me questions, but I could not understand what they were saying. I tried to say something, but my voice center was disabled. My comprehension returned as they talked of transporting me to the local hospital. I shook my head, and Becky told them she would get me to my doctor. As the paramedics departed, I leaned against the wall and cried hard because I knew that the seizures were going to haunt me for the rest of my life.

My doctor took responsibility for the seizure and did not report me to the state department of motor vehicles, which I had feared. As medication was reintroduced, my ability to drive was suspended for thirty days to allow the medication to become fully effective, and we were assured the seizures were controlled once more. I was able to continue working as a construction manager and had support from my supervisor. We adjusted back to the side effects of the medication as my brain processing and my speech slowed down slightly.

A few years later, a complex partial seizure happened while I was with a friend.* I lost consciousness and began to walk out of the building we were in. He became apprehensive as I failed to respond to his questions and my face become distorted. He grabbed my arm as I unknowingly walked towards a very busy street, saving my life. Several hours later, my friend still looked as white as a ghost as he had never witnessed someone have a seizure before. His lack of knowledge about my seizures and his ignorance of what to do to help contributed to his fear.

For me, being reported to the state and losing my driver's license was as stressful, if not more, than having a seizure. Becoming isolated due to lack of transportation was my greatest fear, so much so that when a seizure happened, it wasn't unusual for me to have thoughts of suicide, although I never attempted. I could tell the doctor about having an aura, but not say anything about losing consciousness because it would require him to report me to the state, and my license would automatically be suspended. Without the license, I would lose my job or only be allowed to "sharpen pencils." I never told the whole truth until The Health Insurance Portability and Accountability Act (HIPPA) came into

---

* See appendix C for description and more details about the types of seizures.

effect in 1996, which prohibited doctors from sharing medical information with the state in most circumstances.

There were several occasions when I was the first responder to someone having a seizure. Both occurred in a classroom in front of large groups of people. The first time the seizure lasted 30 seconds and the instructor asked me to tend to the person. Maybe I was one of the few who didn't have fear written all over their faces. The second came a few years later in another classroom. The person sitting next to me slipped into a grand mal seizure. For over two minutes, they were completely stiff, every muscle in their body was convulsing and they couldn't breathe so they were turning blue. All I could do was cradle their head to stop it from pounding against the back of their chair and made sure emergency services were notified. Fortunately, the seizure stopped, and they recovered in the infirmary. The thirty-five other people in the room at the time also needed first aid. Most were in shock; the instructor couldn't move or speak for nearly an hour. It was a good lesson about helping in a traumatic situation through the empathy developed, as I was a person living with epilepsy. It gave meaning to my experiences.

Chapter 5

My marriage to Becky was going well, and we were excited about having a family. The design of our home was great for young children, and within a year of moving in, we were blessed with a healthy son, Bryan. Even at the age of two, he worried about his dad. Often when I had a seizure, which he saw only once, I would clap my hands. Some of his first words were "Uh-oh, Daddy" as I tried to kill a fly by clapping it between my hands. He was scared his father was having a seizure.

With twelve years of experience in construction, I became a project manager and oversaw the design and construction of many significant projects. My level of responsibility increased at home and work, along with my stress level, triggering absence seizures every few years. These involved a loss of consciousness, swallowing hard, and staring; it was not unusual for me to clap or pound my hands. My neurologist increased my treatment from one to two medications; the difficulty was finding the right combination effective in preventing the seizures without changing my personality. There were situations in which I should have been elated, yet I was angry or sad. My ability to recognize the changes and keep my neurologist informed was a blessing.

There was one-time Bryan made me angry because he had learned to run and was doing so in the house. It was one of those moments where I should have been filled with joy over the child's ability, but it overwhelmed me with anger. Fortunately, before I let my emotions overwhelm me and hurt Bryan, I contacted my neurologist straightaway, and was directed to stop taking the medication immediately. Another medication was available, and my old self returned. A week later Bryan started running and squealing with happiness again. This time I was filled with a fatherly joy and

I cheered him on. The neurologist worked hard to help me retain control of the seizures, allowing me to keep my job and be a good husband and father too.

Over the next thirteen years, I was treated with several combinations of medications; some worked well for a few years, and some changed my personality or incapacitated my ability to think and function. Eventually, my seizures increased in intensity and frequency no matter what medication I was on. The toughest part was not knowing when the next seizure would come.

They were like intense storms; sometimes it felt like I was only at the outer edges, fearful of what could happen if they continued to come, then only to watch them fade away without a loss of my consciousness. The most terrifying seizures were the ones that stripped me of any control, like a nor'easter, where I would be thrown into darkness wondering if survival is possible, left only at the mercy of the storm. Days would come when such a storm struck, leaving vivid scars of trauma burned deep in my memory. Facing and recovering from each was a battle within myself.

Bryan and his younger brother, Jason, were teenagers when a seizure happened as I was driving them home in our truck from a camping trip. My foot went down on the gas pedal as the seizure ravaged my brain, and I lost consciousness. Bryan, who was fourteen at the time, took his seatbelt off, slid across the front seat, and managed to knock my foot off the accelerator. He placed his foot on the brake, bringing us to a screeching halt just in front of some large trees at the end of the road. Seeing how close my boys came to possibly being severely injured in an accident tore a hole through my soul as I realized I could no longer be the father my boys needed. I began to have feelings of isolation, along with severe depression caused by the dread of having seizures.

To make things worse, several seizures would occur where my vision would return while in the midst of the storm in my brain, allowing me to see what was happening. I fought harder against the seizures as I saw the panic in my friends and family members. But it was just what the storms wanted. Such mental battles increased the stress that fed the seizures instead of defeating them. The many types of responses people had to my seizures have been etched in my brain. These were based on seeing the distress in their faces or screaming for help. Then there were those who became my heroes. They knew what to do and kept themselves together. They did what was needed for me to quit fighting and focus on recovering by providing me the lifeline I needed to ride out the storms.

My struggle continued for two more years, and I often did not tell my neurologist about the number of partial seizures experienced because I didn't keep a record and my memory was getting poorer; or maybe it was just because I did not want to face reality. A key trigger to the seizures was the shorter days and temperature changes in the Fall, exacerbated by the increase in stress from school starting and work. I had gone through twenty-seven years of treatment when medication was no longer effective, and several partial seizures were now occurring each week. I called my neurologist often, and I was told the only treatment left was to take more of a medication. The side effects were destroying my memory and causing damage to my liver and kidneys. Finally, my neurologist said during the last emergency call, "Matt, I'm sorry. There is nothing else I can do for you. You must call the Epilepsy Center at Johns Hopkins. It is one of the finest throughout the world. Talk to the staff to get an appointment and use me as your referral. I wish you the best."

Anger and loss swept through me as I hung up the phone. I cried out to God, "Why is this happening? Why can't I be the man and father I have the potential of being?" My twenty-year contract with God was over, forgetting that He never signed it. I broke down and cried while sitting in my cubicle as my coworkers listened. They felt sorry for me because they knew something was happening. My ability to complete any work was diminishing, destroying what was left of my positive attitude. To cover for myself, I made up a story about a family member who was struggling with epilepsy because I was scared how my coworkers would react if they knew I was really referring to myself.

It would take a few days before I had the emotional ability to make the phone call to Johns Hopkins. I struggled to answer their basic questions about my history as I felt the hopelessness of my situation sink deeper as I faced reality. Unlike any other part of the body, the brain is who we are. It contains the love we have for others, our personality, and our soul. A magnetic resonance imaging (MRI) was ordered, which provided great detail through the cross-sectional pictures of my brain spaced five millimeters apart. During my first appointment at Johns Hopkins, the neurologist pulled up the MRI and saw layers of lesions (scar tissue) throughout the left hippocampus section, the data processing center of the brain and the source of my seizures.

As he showed me the details, he said, "These are the trigger points of your seizures. Surgery is recommended because we know that medications are no longer effective in your case. Surgery will include taking out a section of your left temporal lobe to allow access for the removal of most, if not all, of your left hippocampus. I cannot tell you at this stage how the surgery will affect your personality. In most cases, the removal of the hippocampus that is damaged will have little impact on your abilities. Apparently, yours is not very functional, and your brain has compensated for some of the loss. However, we do have a series of tests to run you through, and you can call off the surgery at any time. Recovery from the surgery takes about two years."

I felt a sense of relief and terror while listening to his diagnosis and recommendations. He then said, "Let's do a simple test. Tell me, who is the President of the United States?"

I looked at him for a moment, then stared at the floor as I responded, "I know it, but cannot recall it." I then agreed, without reservation, to proceed with the surgery, feeling like the seizures were killing me; maybe not physically, but emotionally, they had won. I refused to give up the fight as I said, "Let's do it!"

The tests were to occur over the next four months so appropriate evaluations could be completed before proceeding with the next test and eventually the surgery. The most important was a week-long EEG evaluation while living in the hospital. The prolonged EEG would provide data on the types of seizures, their source within the brain, and the impact to my cognitive abilities and recovery.

The EEG was the most difficult to endure, even more than the surgery, because I could not leave the room and had no privacy due to constantly being videotaped so my seizures could be evaluated by a team of doctors. Learning about the extent of my seizure disorder caused my self-confidence to be destroyed. Each day, more seizures occurred with the intensity increasing as the medication was decreased. I learned about the intensity of PTSD because for years, I had flashbacks of the seizures and being locked in the confines of a single room. When this happened I became immobilized and began to sweat and tremble. Twelve years later, they would come back to haunt me once again. The memory is vivid and I can replay the details of every moment.

It was on a Tuesday morning. After going through the administrative paperwork, Becky and I were escorted to the wing of the hospital where the neurology department was located. The monitoring section was on the seventh floor, and I was nervous and scared as I wondered how extensive my seizures really were.

The main monitoring station was near the elevator lobby, and the individual room entrances could be seen down the hallway behind it. A nurse was waiting for us at the monitoring station and took us to the room assigned to me. As we walked in, I glanced around at what was to be my home for the next seven days. To me, it was a torture chamber, leaving me wondering when the storms would occur in my brain. Walking down this hallway seemed to have happened many times, even though it had occurred only that one time.

In the room, I could see a camera system in the ceiling and there was a bed, a reclining chair, and a bundle of wires at one end. On one side was a small bathroom with a toilet, sink, and shower. There was a clock above the TV, and I noted that it was 11:30 a.m.

I could see another wing of the hospital from the window with an emergency helicopter landing pad on top. I was instilled with fear by feelings of being locked away and left by myself. At 12:30 Becky had to leave to take care of the boys and she felt bad because we still had not seen a neurologist or technician. She kissed me goodbye and assured me she would be back later that evening. She jokingly told me not to leave. I smiled and stayed in the recliner as she left the room. I had been waiting for some time when my anxiety began to increase, and an aura eventually came, overwhelming me. I pushed back on the recliner, so my legs were straight in front of me to prevent any injury. Then my heart raced, nausea started in my chest, and my peripheral vision was gone.

I glanced at the clock; it was exactly 1:00 p.m., and the seizure continued to progress. I lost all awareness for over twenty minutes. My senses started to recover as the storm subsided in my brain and left me wondering where I was. The clock was still right in front of me, as the seizure prevented any movement. I saw that it was 1:20 PM. Nearly another hour passed before I realized I was in a hospital, but I could not recall the name of it. It would take a few more hours before I could remember the name of the hospital and that I was in a room being used to monitor my seizures. My speech was impeded, preventing me from calling out for help.

At 3:30, a neurologist came and the first thing he asked was, "When was the last time you had a seizure?" I told him, "At one o'clock today." He was shocked as I heard him mutter, "I can't believe we missed a seizure!" several times.

He promptly had a technician attach the electrodes to my head, leaving me wired to the wall with a twenty-foot tether. It was now impossible to depart the room and I had no privacy while under constant video surveillance and EEG monitoring. Whenever I felt a seizure come, I needed to push a button to inform the staff. A nurse or technician would then hurry to my room and make sure I did not get hurt or require emergency services. It was comforting to know the medical staff was there in case something did go wrong. Two more auras occurred later that afternoon, this time with no loss of consciousness.

I noticed there was little difference between an aura and a panic attack. With both, there was an increased heart rate and anxiety peaks. Both affected my speech for several hours, as that part of the brain was resetting. I knew what I wanted to say but could not transmit it to my mouth for the words to come out. The auras began with a wave of nausea, and the panic attacks started with a sudden, extremely high feeling of anxiety.

I had been isolated for nearly five days, and the seizures were coming more often with greater intensity as the medication level in my blood decreased. The dosage was minimal, and my liver filtered it out of my blood faster than it was consumed. I had four seizures in the past twenty-four hours, and as I realized the extent of my disorder, depression set in. A friend came to visit and was shocked by what he saw. From his perspective, he saw a close friend who loved to be outdoors now tied in a room with a series of wires attached to his head. He stayed for a little while but had to leave because he was afraid of me having a seizure right in front of him.

That night, as I watched a movie, anxiety set in, and the room seemed to get even smaller. Then there was total darkness, except for the glow of the TV. The anxiety then peaked and wiped out my memory of what to do, hitting the call button became impossible. As the anxiety intensified, the aura came, and the TV screen seemed to get smaller and smaller until it drifted away. When the seizure ended, I started to cry uncontrollably. I felt beaten and had lost hope. Suddenly, there was a man standing in front of me. He did not have the garb of a hospital staffer. He was dressed in plain clothes and wore a large cross in front of him. All he did was hold me close as I sobbed, with the cross between us. When I mentioned this to the staff later, no one knew who he was, but several nurses smiled at me. Officially, I was told this must have been a vision caused by the seizure.

This was my fourteenth seizure in five days. Early the next morning, my neurologist came into the room and told me they had enough data and that I was going home a day early. When Becky came, I gave her a long hug. I did not want to let go, fearing that she would leave without me. She assured me we would be going home soon but would not hold my hand and excused herself from the room, saying she had to talk to the staff. I later learned that she was struggling with PTSD as she had witnessed me have so many seizures, she was afraid of watching me die. She could only imagine the worst-case scenario: her husband completely disabled or dead. For me, I already was, with the restrictions and fears a person struggling with epilepsy must face. Driving restrictions were imposed, limiting my mobility.

Within twenty-four hours, the neurology team recommended a lobectomy (brain surgery) involving the removal of a third of the left temporal lobe to allow access and extraction of most of the hippocampus on the left side. Without doubting for a moment, I elected to have the surgery because my inability to function at work due to loss of memory, inability to drive, and being isolated from my family because of their being afraid of my seizures became intolerable. The seizures now impacted my verbal skills and memory for several days. I was constantly living with the trauma of the seizures and was now battling the apprehension of the outcome of the surgery. *Would I still be the same person, or would my brain be so damaged I would not be able to function?* As it came closer to the surgery date, I wondered, *were they going to cut my soul out of my body?*

It was normal for me to feel enveloped in the past while talking about this. Then I heard several people talking and I saw a few hurry out of the room, and this brought me back to the present. Carol came over and said, "I don't think they can take hearing about the surgery. Some of us just don't do well hearing such details." She had the room lights turned bright and told everyone, "I should let you know that Mr. Johnson is going to talk about his surgery. We understand if some of you need to leave. Let's take a fifteen-minute break." She then turned to me and asked, "I assume this is okay, is it?"

I felt tired but confident and thought back for a moment of the time when being so tired was a trigger to my seizures. I looked at her and said, "The break is a good idea. I need a little rest myself. Thanks for stepping in."

Chapter 6

It was time to get started again, and the auditorium seemed fuller than before. I had guessed a few people wouldn't be able to stomach it, but it seemed the people who had left spread the word to others. When I realized more people were interested in learning about my brain surgery, a calm came over me, just like on the morning it happened. It was time to get started as the room became quiet, and Carol had the lights dimmed.

The day of my lobectomy seemed to start as a routine workday; the alarm clock went off at the regular time, with the basics of showering and getting dressed, followed with waking the boys and seeing them off to school. The major difference that day, however, was that I gave both a hug but did not want to let go, afraid that it would be the last time I would remember who they were. They knew their dad would be headed to the hospital soon, and just like me, they did not want to let go either. I struggled to hold back my tears as our friend picked them up and drove off to school. Then it was time to head to the hospital, and Becky was sad and wished that the surgery was not necessary. Our pastor met us there and prayed with us as we sat in the waiting room.

It is difficult to remember all the details of what happened as it seemed to take forever yet felt like it occurred in an instant. Giving Becky a hug when it was time to get on the gurney in preparation for surgery was even more difficult than saying goodbye to our boys. We didn't want to let go of each other. For her it would be a difficult twelve hours, wondering who her husband would be when it was all over. Her second round of fearful trials in our marriage was about to begin. The first round was the unknowns of the seizures I had, the second was the many years necessary for me to recover from surgery.

I remember laying on the gurney in another room, talking with the anesthesiologist, and signing some document. A mask came over my face and I was told to count backward from a hundred. *Ninety-seven* was the last thing I remember saying before losing consciousness, and my memory was put on hold. It was amazing how the number *one hundred* would play an important role in my recovery a few days later.

The surgery started with the cutting of my hair off along the tract where the incision would be made. The incision started from in front of the bottom of my left ear, then up and around it, then several inches toward the back of my head before going up to the top, then toward the front using the cowlick on my right side as a guide, and stopping at the edge of the hairline. The skin was then pulled down over my face, exposing the skull. A saw was then used to cut out a rectangular section, approximately one-and-a-half inches high and three inches long. It was placed in a special formula to protect the bone from drying which causes the cells to die. This exposed over half of my left temporal lobe. Over a third of the forward section of the lobe was removed, exposing the limbic system, where the hippocampus, the center of my seizures, was located. The hippocampus is responsible for processing long-term memory and emotional response, and in my case, was filled with electrical storms from damaged cells that triggered my seizures and damaged more cells.

The surgeon then removed most of the left hippocampus, leaving a burrowed hole where it extended up toward the top of the central part of my brain. The void created was filled with a fluid, and the section of my skull that had been removed was set back in place. Two nails were driven through the back of my head to keep the section of bone from slipping into the void where part of my brain used to be. Four circular plates with five screws each were attached at the corners to keep the bone in place. Over several years, the bone would grow back together and over the plates.

The skin was then pulled back in place, and the surgeon did such a fantastic job that extraordinarily little scar tissue formed. A biopsy of the hippocampus indicated severe hardening or damage, the result of head injuries and seizures. It also indicated that a little bit more should have been removed. That little section would continue to cause simple seizures that no longer impacted my cognitive abilities but reminded me of the seizures that had terrified and nearly killed me.

I saw Carol looking at me with concern on her face, like she wanted to know if I could continue. I had talked about this so many times that now the words came without any emotions. I smiled to reassure her that everything was okay and continued without pause.

Chapter 7

The surgery was generally successful but with a significant impact to my engineering skills. Math was difficult, remembering names was impossible, and I struggled with basic word recall. The morning after the surgery, several neurologists came into my room. They asked me the same basic questions several times.

"What is your name?"

"How old are you?"

"What day of the week is this?"

"What is your wife's name?"

"Where are you now?"

"What type of hospital is it?"

Fortunately, I could recall my name and especially my wife's. It would take another day for me to remember what day of the week it was, and the facility I was in being a hospital, but I could not remember the name of it. They would tell me "This is Johns Hopkins." When the question was repeated a few minutes later, I still could not recall the name. The neurologist who worked with me in my week of EEG monitoring came several times and was very disappointed I was not improving.

I was given a salad and hamburger later that day for lunch. I bit into the hamburger and could only taste the salt. My sense of taste was temporarily impacted by the surgery and swelling of my brain and salt was the only flavor that registered in my mind. Since it was the only flavor I could identify, it was intensified a hundred times over. I could not find the words necessary to explain my situation making it impossible to verbally respond to Becky or the nurse about my inability to eat.

My neurologist came to see me soon after lunch to check on my progress. After asking me how I was feeling, he said, "What's one hundred minus seven?"

I could not figure out what he meant by one hundred or seven, let alone minus. He must have been able to sense my attempt to recall what he was talking about as he patiently waited, with an expression that buried any concern he may have had. After a few minutes, the number ninety-five popped into my mind. I use the expression "popped into my mind" because my memory at the time was blank, and there was nothing to recall. Imagine someone asking you a question in a foreign language, and you have no idea what they were saying, then suddenly the answer comes, not in your language, but in theirs.

Ninety-five seemed to register with the question asked, so I said, "Ninety-five." Suddenly, I felt that it was incorrect and said, "No, that's not right." Another minute went by, and the number *ninety-three* popped into my mind, "It is ninety-three," I said.

The doctor then asked, "What is ninety-three minus seven?"

Again, I was baffled, then suddenly the number *eight* then *eighty-eight* came to mind, it's, "Eighty-eight." There was this sensation that *eighty-eight* was not correct, however, and then I corrected myself by saying, "No, that's not right." The *number eighty-six* suddenly appeared in my mind and seemed correct, even though my immediate thought was *What is eighty-six?* I then said, "Eighty-six."

The doctor asked, "What is eighty-six minus seven?"

My mind suddenly could recall all the numbers starting with *eight*, from *eighty* to *eighty-nine*. Taking *seven* away from *eighty-six* was less than *eighty*, but what was the number before *eighty*? After what seemed like forever, the *seventies* came, and I answered, "Seventy-nine."

The doctor said, "Minus seven."

My brain was stressed, and I was getting tired. The number *seventy-two* came to mind quickly.

"Minus seven."

I could not recall the sequence of numbers that came before the *seventies*. Then the number *sixty-five* came, and I answered. The moment I answered, I heard "Minus seven." The number *sixty* was not enough, and suddenly the number *fifty-eight* registered, "Fifty-eight."

"Minus seven."

I immediately said, "Fifty-one."

"Minus seven."

By this time, my head was severely aching, and I was exhausted. After we got to and I said, "forty-four," the doctor said it was time to take a break, and I immediate went to sleep. I didn't know at that time, that years later, I would use this technique to help a neighbor try to recover her mathematical skills lost to a stroke.

The pain from the surgery was unbearable, and a system to self-apply the pain medication was explained to me. When the pain reached intolerable levels, I called the staff. My inability to remember how to apply the medication became a concern for them, and the psychology department was called to perform a test of my cognitive skills and memory. The test was relatively simple and consisted of pictures of items someone of my background should easily identify. The ones I could not answer were the ones associated with engineering. I recognized them but could not find the name of the objects, indicating significant memory issues. When it came to name recall, I did well with family members; I could not, however, remember the name of my neurologist or surgeon or the name of the hospital. I felt dumb, and the pain in my head became intense. The technician would not allow any pain medication until the test was complete as it would impact my memory.

The technician then told Becky I needed extensive therapy that would start in a couple of weeks. We were both speechless.

Becky, because this was never expected, and me because I was not able to find the words necessary to express myself, as they were in my memory somewhere. Recovery did not entail relearning; it required rewiring to access the memory in the forward part of my brain. Somehow, I knew the only way to do so was to develop a need to recall information and never quitting when I couldn't. I never needed the therapist, but what happened that day caused a huge scar in Becky's relationship with me.

The assistant chief of the food services came to see me a few hours before our leaving the hospital. She wanted my opinion about the food and their services. It took a while for me to come up with an answer to her question because my way of thinking as an engineer had always provided examples when describing my position on an issue. This time, my brain could not assemble the words to appropriately express this. I could imagine what should have been said, but the words just weren't there. Finally, after a few minutes and seeing her expression of concern, I said, "It sucks."

It was nice to hear the audience laugh.

Chapter 8

The neurologist said that recovery from surgery would take two years, and I was learning that he was correct as far as the seizures were concerned. Two weeks after surgery, the seizures were occurring several times a day, but the difference being I never lost consciousness. Agoraphobia set in, the fear of everything. It was necessary to have years of exposure to people and work settings to overcome it. I did not realize how intense recovery would be and that full mental and emotional recovery would take nearly *ten* years.

The men at the church I attended played a key role in my recovery. They prayed for me, came to my house when Becky had to go to work, and challenged me to recover. To get over my agoraphobia, they had me lead the prayer part of the service on Sundays. Writing a three-minute prayer took me hours. The anxiety involved in standing in front of fifty people caused my body to tremble but gave me the exposure necessary to overcome the fear and regain control. This went on for several years. A healthy nervousness still lingers today. Eventually, my role expanded to include sermons and running the entire service on occasion. Prayer no longer takes as much time to prepare anymore as it now comes naturally. God was working through an entire congregation to demonstrate how He makes us stronger through faith.

After I developed confidence that my fears could be defeated, a complex partial seizure came during my sleep, reminding me that the battle was not over. The potential triggers were simple and associated with leave from work and going on travel, the change of environment, dehydration, excitement, and stress. Only this time, the trigger was a decrease in stress by being away from work. EMTs were called because I was turning blue from shortness of breath, and oxygen was given to help in my recovery.[*] The biggest difference from the seizures occurring before surgery and those after was that my recovery time was significantly shorter. All my cognitive functions returned within minutes, and my memory which used to require days to recover, now only took a few hours. The second seizure occurred about six months later, a year after the surgery. This one started in my sleep and woke me up.

Let me explain what such a seizure is like: It was a Sunday morning, and I was on the second day of a vacation at the beach with my family. The triggers were basically the same as all my seizures. I was awakened by a wave of nausea, I could feel my heart racing, and was filled with anxiety, like I was about to take a final exam— only much more intense. I got out of bed and walked to the kitchen and got a drink of water. My thought at the time was, this was happening because I was dehydrated from being outside in the summer heat the day before. Although I had slept for over seven hours, I felt exhausted and went back to bed and fell into a deep sleep.

The nausea associated with the preictal stage woke me up again an hour later. Still believing this to be caused by dehydration, I felt it best to get another drink. As my feet hit the floor, I lost consciousness as the seizure swept through my entire brain. I fell and my head hit the corner of the nightstand. I laid on the floor for quite a while, shaking as all the muscles in my body contracted, like what happens when you hold a heavy object for several minutes. My front teeth clenched my tongue, and blood was dribbling out of my mouth. This went on for approximately twenty minutes, and through a part of it, I had an awareness of what was happening even though all my senses were impacted and nonfunctional. Imagine you were frozen in a block of ice with your eyes closed. You cannot see, hear, touch, breath, speak, or move, but you know something is happening. As the ice melts, different senses are reactivated, and

---

[*] EMT stands for emergency medical technician

you regain control of your body parts. Then like a computer, your brain begins to reset.

The first of my senses to return was my vision, and I could see my son talking to a paramedic. I could not move my eyes or hear or feel anything. As I was picked up and put on the gurney and loaded into the ambulance it felt like I was watching it happening on TV with the volume off—no sense of touch or ability to hear what was happening. I was transported to the hospital. Along the way, my senses began to return, yet I could not talk. Over and over again, I heard the EMT say "What is your name?" It would not be until reaching the hospital that I could say "Matt," but nothing more.

The doctors immediately believed the seizure was caused by an illegal drug overdose; a conclusion typical of the staff in most hospitals. They would not listen to me or my family. Their attitude enforced the stigma I carried and many of us living with epilepsy. They ran a CAT scan of my head and some blood tests to find out what drug I used which validated what my family told them was true. The attitudes of the staff and their method of treatment suddenly changed. I was given another dosage of my epilepsy medication and was treated for the injuries to my face from the fall. There was nothing more they could do for the injuries in my mouth and the torn muscles throughout my body caused by the seizure. After several hours, they determined there was a low risk to me having another seizure, and we were sent home. The most difficult part to deal with was my walking due to the pain from the tears in the muscles. The pain lasted for several weeks and was a constant reminder I was losing the war, or so I thought.

This was my last complex seizure, although I have come close to losing consciousness a few times after that as the auras still come—sometimes with great intensity but then they go no further. I never really lost consciousness again afterwards. Even so, this seizure broke my heart, coming after the surgery and as I realized its impact to my mental abilities. The feeling of defeat lasted for months. It was my faith and family that kept me going and restored my drive to refuse to quit trying or to give up hope. There had to be a reason and a plan God had for all this.

I learned to live with my disabilities and was surprised by all the people who supported and motivated me to heal. In fact, the disabilities were helping me associate with other people living in similar situations. New windows were opening for the future, and the demand on my brain increased my memory's recovery. As the healing continued, the seizures decreased to once a month, lasting only for a few seconds, and the best part was, they were simple focal seizures, and I never lost consciousness anymore.

The reason for my struggle with epilepsy and surgery was realized four years after surgery. I was at work talking with a gentleman who lived several hours away about scheduling a meeting. He told me he would not be available the next week because he was going on a make-a-wish trip with his son; then he said, "My son has epilepsy."

That's when I went dead quiet for more than a minute as I struggled with what to say. *Should I tell him about myself or keep quiet?* The words of my father kept coming to me: "Never tell anyone!" I decided to keep quiet about my experience. With the phone being silent for so long, he thought I'd hung up on him, which had happened regularly to him in the past when he told people his story. He and his family had faced rejection many times because of his child's seizures. Then he heard me say, "Your son and I have much in common."

The child was four, had intractable seizures, and had a lobectomy to try and help him to regain control. As I shared my story, I heard him say "But you're a project manager! This cannot be." During the ensuing conversation, he learned about seizure triggers from the perspective of a person actually struggling with them. Many of his caregiver perspectives changed as he learned how his son could still hear while having a seizure and that the reflection of the sun off a swimming pool could serve as a trigger for them. One day, I received a letter from his wife, thanking me for giving them hope. That letter inspired me to share hope with other people. Soon after, I volunteered to be a mentor with the Epilepsy Foundation.

My experiences with epilepsy and work as a project manager provided me a gifted ability to help others, and led to my going to graduate school to pursue a degree in pastoral counseling. My disabilities were both a hindrance and a blessing, as I discovered by nearly failing out of my first class. Answering fill-in-the-blank type of questions was impossible because that ability was controlled through the part of the brain that had been removed. However, the professor was willing and able to help because his mother suffered with seizures, so he understood some of my challenges. Challenging my brain this way made it rewire even more. After four years of studies and work, I no longer needed disability services. It had been eight years since my surgery and the follow-on traumas. My self-esteem was reestablished, and I felt whole once again.

I had a mini epiphany about my experience a few weeks before finishing my last class. A person named Jessica came up to me and introduced herself. She was a semester behind me and wanted to thank me for the example I had set that provided her the motivation to complete the program. She told me, "A few years ago, I was about to quit because my memory was not good enough to get me through the classes. When I told the professor about leaving, he told me about you and your persevering through his course. Just knowing that there was someone else like me, who had struggled with seizures and brain surgery, and was in the program gave me the inspiration needed to believe that I could do it too. I kept wanting to meet you, but our classes have never been on the same day of the week until now."

I kept looking at her with feelings of disbelief and amazement. Then she said, "Can I give you a hug? You reminded me that I am not alone and how God works through people who should be broken." That is when I came out of my state of shock and nodded while fighting back the tears. We gave each other a hug. That was something special as we knew that God's amazing grace had been working through both of us. I wished her the best and asked if I could come to her graduation. She smiled and said, "I would greatly appreciate it."

Working full-time and going to graduate school proved to be an extensive load on my brain. This induced the need for it to rewire to enable my memory to function better. Overall, my recovery from brain surgery took more than nine years and will probably continue as long as I challenge my brain. All along, it was clear that God was sending people who could help me and whom I could help by sharing our stories and experiences.

My degree enabled me to become a full-time counselor, providing the opportunity for me to retire from my career as an engineer. I worked for several years with people dealing with brain injury and epilepsy. My work was effective because of my ability to relate to the clients through my experience of living with seizures and with the side-effects of medications. However, there were times I would have flashbacks of my seizures and visits to the hospital, along with being locked in a room for extended EEG monitoring, and the days after surgery when I could not remember the name of the hospital. It's difficult going into any hospital now as it triggers flashbacks to the times of my walking down the corridors or into the rooms at Johns Hopkins. It became even more difficult a few years later.

Regrettably, the stress of the surgery and recovery traumatized my wife, and she could not recover. She had watched me have too many seizures and lived with the impact the surgery had on my character. She was locked in her survival mode of emotions and was never able to return to the role of being my best friend and lover. We decided divorce would be best.

It was time for change, a time away from my work and the reminders of the ones I lost. The stress of living in a bustling metropolitan area added to my anxiety. I needed a quieter place to live, where it provided distance from my work and past experiences for a while. After weeks of searching, I discovered the perfect place and moved away to the quiet little town of Creeksville on the eastern shore. It is on one of the river tributaries, with access to boating, wonderful fishing, and being away from my past. Or so I thought. My calling as a mentor and counselor was about to be tested to the extreme.

At this point I felt a sense of closure within myself. The room was totally silent, and it took a moment for me to realize that it was not empty, and this was validated when the lights were turned brighter. I could see the clock in the back of the room and realized we were running late. Then Carol came over to talk about the next session. "We will meet here tomorrow at 10 a.m. I recommend you come back because if you were amazed by what you learned today, it gets even better tomorrow."

She then smiled at me and said, "You'll be here at nine-thirty, won't you?"

I affirmed by smiling and nodding. I was tired and had had enough for the day. I won the battle by facing some of those most distressing times of my past yet maintaining control of myself.

I had been standing for several hours and needed a quiet place to rest my legs. Several people came down to thank me, and a few wanted to talk some more. But I was tired of standing. Carol told me of a room down the hall where we could meet and rest for a minute. A few other people who had attended the seminar also knew of this place. They saw me and came over to our table, asking if they could join us. Everyone wanted to know more about my experience, and we talked for a while.

Sidney brought up the part about people's misconception of seizures. "I really appreciated what you said about how you were treated while in the hospital. I was arrested twice while having a seizure. I have no memory of what happened during the seizure, only regaining consciousness in a jail cell where I had a black eye and one of my teeth was knocked out. Apparently, I had slapped an officer, hitting him pretty hard, and his reaction lead to my injuries. Not being allowed my medication led to another seizure the next day. That's when the police realized I was not lying about my condition and allowed me to call my wife who was very upset I'd not been in contact and had reported me missing to the police. On our way out, I met the officer I unknowingly slapped and apologized to him. He felt bad and apologized to me too. It is nice to know I'm not alone in all this. Thank you."

As we were getting up to leave, another person said, "You have talked about epilepsy all day. Can you tell us when you will talk about people who have had a stroke?"

I turned to look at him and said, "Tomorrow." He responded, "Thank you. My mother had a stroke last week, so your talk is very important and personal to us."

When he said this, a shot of anxiety ran through me, and I could not respond. It continued to intensify while walking down the hallway, then an aura started. I knew I had to quickly change my environment, or it would get worse, leaving me fearful. I quickened my pace until I was nearly running out of the building to my car. As the building door closed behind me, the aura subsided, but part of the anxiety remained. Reliving the past turned out to be tougher than I expected.

There was a park near my hotel with a clear area where I could see the sky. Walking through the park and watching the sunset enabled my mind to overcome the fear, and a calmness returned; a spiritual moment that enabled me to have peace, knowing I was never alone.

Section II

New Beginnings

On Tuesday morning, I felt nervous about the day and prayed that all would go well. Knowing a little more about the audience would be helpful to me, so I arrived early and took a seat at the back of the auditorium, watching the people come into the room. There was a lot of chatter, and I caught a few comments about what they learned the previous day. I knew it was time to start when I heard someone say "What got me was he went through that surgery and is able to talk to us like he did yesterday. He doesn't even have notes to remember what to say." Some were sharing their experience about living with epilepsy, while others talked of their roles in caring for someone in need.

There was someone new to the group who was in a wheelchair with a person kneeling in front of them. I hurried down to meet them and get some of their story before getting started. Knowing they had not been to the previous session, I proceeded to introduced myself. The lady in the wheelchair was Helen, and she had a stroke several weeks earlier. Her son, Mark, who looked familiar, was with her. He looked exhausted and I realized he was in the discussion group the day before. Seeing him reminded me of my experience with my neighbor. Helen smiled as she started to share her story about her stroke. She seemed to have done well, then Mark said, "She's not motivated to get better as she should be out of the wheelchair by now. I'm hoping that what she hears today will make her work harder."

Carol came over to me and asked, "Are you ready?" I nodded and headed to the podium as she began to introduce me. Talking with Mark and Helen pulled me backed into the darkness of the past making me need something to physically hold on to for support. I learned that a tight grip helped reel in the nervousness and allowed me to retain reality. Carol then said, "Mr. Johnson is going to talk about someone he met who suffered from a stroke. Please give him a round of applause."

Carol's introduction and a delay in getting the auditorium lights dimmed provided the time I needed to bring my thoughts together. My nerves calmed down as the memories of sharing faith and hope was so involved throughout this story, it now felt natural to speak to everyone.

Chapter 9

My new home was along the eastern shore in an older neighborhood, a house with more than fifty years of wear and tear. Even though it needed many repairs and renovations, it had a covered area to store a fishing boat and a small barn in the back I could rebuild for a shop and storage. Access to the water was a few minutes away with a very nice boat ramp and parking area for free, and marinas for larger boats were close by too. It seemed like heaven because some of the best sailing and fishing was literally down the street. It made me feel safe because it eliminated the stress of living near a metropolitan area. Everything was quiet and peaceful. The people were friendly, even strangers smiled and waved at me as they passed by.

To make this easier, my older sister, Jennifer, with whom I have a very close relationship, lived in the same town. No matter what was going on in our lives, the other was there to lend a hand or provide a hug or was simply there to talk with and get a new perspective. Our relationship was even tighter than ever due to the traumas we've both experienced in our lives and the fact we have always been there for each other. Now I had nothing to worry about concerning backup support and friendship, even if a seizure were to occur.

The house was a great help in getting me recharged from my past as it challenged me in installing new doors, windows, flooring, and bathroom fixtures. I came up with a color scheme that centered on the beach and being near the water—with blue, green, and brown colors, making the home comfortable to my standards.

Soon after moving in, my nephew Tim contacted me. He had made a living as a pro fisherman and shared how the area was one of the highest-rated regions for fishing on the east coast. When I learned how good the fishing was it made me want to get out on the river where the fish were waiting to be caught. Shopping for a used pickup truck and a bass boat became a top priority.

Without much effort, I found a 20-year-old pickup that fit my needs with a long bed and extra storage behind the front seats. It did not take long for me to find a twenty-five-year-old bass boat that was fifteen feet long with a ninety-horsepower engine. It was older than my youngest child, yet in wonderful condition. The boat was very stable and had a set of seats to sit low in the cockpit while driving fast. There were pedestal seats near the bow and stern for two people to fish from. I now had everything I needed to go fishing, except knowing where the fish were and what to use for bait.

After telling Tim of my truck and boat, he hurried over to spend the weekends with me. To get everything fitted out properly, he brought the latest rods and lures and shared how and when to use each. Of course, he always kept the best for himself by not giving me all the secrets as it seemed he always caught the first and the biggest fish. This would eventually change as I learned more of his techniques while quietly watching him.

His knowledge of the various boat ramps and fishing spots where the bass and the drum, the greatest tasting yet hardest fish to catch were found was most important. We had to be in the boat at his secret fishing places prior to sunrise, which meant leaving the house by four or five in the morning. We would fish along the bay and tributaries within fifty miles of home. My dinner menu quickly changed to include the many fish we caught.

Early in the morning, we would use surface baits, those that floated, and he taught me how to cast and jerk the bait along to attract the fish. The fish would try to catch the bait yet often would miss due to poor vision or timing; it was most important to keep the lure moving so they would try again. Often it was their second or third attempt that enabled us to set the hook and reel them in. As the sun rose and the day got warmer, the fish would go deep, and we would change our lures to the ones that sank and moved along within a few feet of the bottom.

The big question was where are the fish and will they strike our bate. It could take twenty to thirty casts before we found them. On other days, we landed one that was twenty to thirty inches long on the first cast, large enough to meet the limit and take home. He taught me the importance of being ready for the fish to strike and made jokes when the fish were not interested in being caught or had gone to another place to feed. There was always the blessing of the morning sky with its rainbow colors and being surrounded by the wonders of Mother Nature, whether the fish wanted to join us or not.

Building up the courage and the belief that I could take the fishing boat out by myself required experience, taking the risk, and believing in myself. I struggled with the fear of having a seizure and its consequences when out in the boat, often leaving me filled with doubt, but I was determined to conquer it through my love of God's creation and being on the water.

Many of my dreams were coming true, yet I had no one with the same level of interest to share them with. My work on the home and fishing kept me busy, and my body was improving in strength and endurance. Developing techniques to do a three-person job by myself was a challenge that required not just engineering skills but also much creativity and application of many parts of my brain. I was given an avenue to meet people and stay busy through obtaining the materials and asking others how they would accomplish some of the complex work. Being on the water made me feel closer to nature and to God. But something was missing from my little heaven on earth.

Chapter 10

I knew it was time to enter the part of the story about the stroke and resulting brain injury my friend Sara experienced, and I required a pause to get my emotions in check. I stared at the floor for a minute before continuing. It was time to share her story, which had been impossible without tears coming down my face until recently. I knew as a counselor how talking about a traumatic event develops a new perspective of what happened and an ability to live with it. Just maybe this time, I could get through it. I took a deep breath, cleared my throat, and continued.

A few months after moving into my new home, someone moved into the house next door. As I came out of my workshop one day, my new neighbor shouted "Hello" to me as she came across her backyard to introduce herself. As I saw her coming, I walked over to the chain-linked fence between our yards to talk to her. She was my height and had a beaming smile. Her hair was gray and short. Her eyes were blue and sparkly. Her voice was appealing as she introduced herself as Sara and asked, "What's your name?"

She was excited about being in the area, and we soon began talking about the work we were doing. Within a few minutes, my excitement grew as we had so much in common. She was on her second career as a pastor of a church nearby and had recently graduated with a degree in Divinity. Of course, I had recently graduated and earned my license to be a pastoral counselor. Her mission was to work with a body of people; mine focused on individuals.

As we discussed why we picked our second-career fields, Sara told me how for years, she had attended church and worked with people. She had been a social worker, helping children in families where hunger, abuse, and addictions were common. As she talked of this, I thought of the people I had worked with, who were suffering from drug and alcohol addictions brought on by abuse. Sara was a walking miracle, having suffered a severe hemorrhagic stroke six months earlier that had paralyzed the left side of her body and compromised her ability to speak and eat.[*]

In less than a month, she was able to walk and had regained 70 percent of her left arm functions. Her face was no longer distorted, and her mouth was fully functional with no impact or distortion to her speech. I was amazed at our similarities with work, careers, family, health experiences, and spiritual callings. I felt totally at ease and knew she was someone who could easily relate to and comprehend my experiences. The amazing part was that I learned all this through our introductory discussion of less than ten minutes. I thought, *How could someone with such similar life experiences become my next-door neighbor?* We would have talked longer, but Sara had to leave to guide her moving company in placing her furniture. As she stepped away, she said, "I hope to talk to you again soon. There is something special in our being neighbors." I just stood at the fence, grinning, and watching her until she disappeared back into her house. Before leaving the yard, I quietly asked myself, *Was this a dream, or did this really happen?*

A few days later, I saw Sara outside, playing with her retriever. Her dog, Samuel, saw me coming into her yard and came straight at me with his teeth bared and was growling. I kept coming forward, knowing how showing fear would lead to his biting me. Instead, he nipped at my foot, drawing a little blood. He then placed himself between Sara and me with his teeth bared and growling loudly. Sara yelled at him, "Samuel! That is Matt. He is a friend!"

---

[*] Hemorrhagic strokes consist of severe bleeding in the brain. There is less than a 25 percent probability someone would survive, even less that they could fully recover.

Samuel then came back toward me, this time with his tail wagging and rubbing up against me. Sara was apologizing, telling me how Samuel protected her from people he didn't know.

I smiled at Sara and said, "I am a very nice person and safe to be around," while rubbing Samuel under the chin.

Sara responded, "I don't know about that, but I would like to learn more," with a huge smile and a sparkle in her eyes. Her presence just made me feel good.

The two of us saw each other on a regular basis, if only to say "Hi" or to talk more about our calling in the ministries. Overall, we were open with each another, and I got to know a few of the members of the church where she was the pastor. I felt blessed and fulfilled in my house now because of my new neighbor. The more we got to talk to each other, the more we found things in common, and she was amazed by my experience with epilepsy and was excited knowing about my love of the water. She loved to go sailing whenever she could on the bigger boats where she could live for several days. She had many tales to tell about her experiences on the high seas.

She told me about her shopping for homes and selecting the one next to mine. It was the perfect size for her with a yard for Samuel and within ten minutes of where she worked. As we learned more about each other, we both felt a strong sense of divine intervention in our coming together. Although we both had suffered much with brain injury and family separation, which often happens in such situations, it was our positive attitudes, faith, and drive to overcome such difficult circumstances that created an instant bond. Every time she saw me, her face lit up with a smile and her eyes sparkled as she looked deep into mine. I felt a sense of joy, like we had known each other for years.

Chapter 11

It was a Thursday evening, and I was about to sit down to eat dinner when my doorbell rang. As I opened the front door and flipped on the light, I saw Sara standing on the porch. She was dressed in an old pair of jeans and a sweatshirt, as she had not planned to leave her house until the next day. I invited her in and saw the worried look on her face. She looked at me and asked, "What is happening to my eyes?" As I watched them, she said, "I tossed a ball down the hallway for Samuel to retrieve, then saw him do it again and again. It seemed weird at first because when I saw him do it again, the ball was in my hand and he was sitting beside me."

While I listened to her story, I noticed her eyes were going back and forth arrhythmically. At one point, she was cross-eyed; a moment later, her eyes were looking in opposite directions. I immediately recognized what was happening and told her, "You are having a seizure, and we need to get you to the hospital immediately." I remained calm but wondered if her seizure had been caused by another stroke that may be occurring or part of the healing process from her previous stroke.

In spite of how she felt, she said, "Oh no, we can't. I see your dinner on the table, and you need to eat. Once you have finished, then we can go." She sat down at the table and tried to point to my dinner, saying, "You shared the importance of your not skipping meals, so please eat. You need to take care of yourself." She even smiled as she continued, "I sure don't need you to have a seizure too."

I ate very quickly, and after she had me put the dishes in the sink, we headed for my car. We sped down the highway well over the speed limit because of my fear of what was happening intensified. As we approached the hospital, she said, "I'm scared.

Can you stay with me?" I assured her I would as we pulled up to the emergency room entrance.

I jumped out of the car and found a wheelchair near the door. Sara had some difficulty getting out of the car, and as soon as she was in the wheelchair, we quickly headed to the emergency room entry. Once we were in the building, the security officer told me to move my car to the parking lot. A nurse came quickly, assuring me Sara was safe and enabling me to relocate the car. My adrenaline level was very high at this point and running back into the hospital helped burn some of it off. Her seizure seemed simple, yet I was concerned it would spread to other areas of the brain as mine had. She never lost consciousness and was able to answer all the questions the hospital staff asked as they registered her in their computer system. She smiled at me and whispered, "Thank you" several times.

It was very late when she was admitted for evaluation. When she was comfortable, I told her I'd be back in the morning. It was easy for me to stay awake while driving home because of the frustration I felt with what had happened. One of my reasons for moving to the eastern shore was to take a break from my work caring for people struggling with epilepsy. Now my next-door neighbor had had a seizure. A few times, I said out loud, "This just sucks," then assured myself it was just an episode. *Let it go.* I was exhausted upon arriving home, so dwelling upon what happened was nearly impossible. Sleep came quickly.

Overnight, Sara was monitored with a continuous EEG and was very surprised to see me, even though I had promised to check on her the next day. It was mentally challenging for me to be in hospitals, sometimes triggering PTSD and, in worse cases, a partial seizure. This time the PTSD came as I noticed the hallway appearance suddenly change. The local hospital was gone, and it turned into Johns Hopkins, like I was approaching the room where my extended EEG took place. The lighting suddenly became brighter and the hallway significantly wider and looked newer. I could not tell if the people were real or part of the vision I was having. My heart was racing. I was brought back to reality as I got closer to Sara's room, and I returned to the reality of being in the local hospital, with the dimmer lighting. A wave of nausea surged through my body, as the preictal stage of my complex partial seizures came on, then only to fade away without impacting my cognitive abilities. My hand was trembling noticeably while reaching for the door to her room. A battle was underway in my mind to overcome a strong sense of anxiety, a remnant of the simple focal seizure I just experienced.

Sara smiled as I entered the room and was flattered to see me, even though she was in hospital garb and her hair a mess with a bunch of EEG wires sticking out. She had not even been able to wash her face that morning. She explained how well she was and excited about being able to go home later in the day.

My smile faded as she said, "The doctors told me the EEG is indicating a continuous seizure in a part of my brain, but that it is okay because it does not impact my ability to think or do anything, although it may impact my vision for a while. It is centralized in the back of my brain where the stroke occurred. They put me on some seizure medication, and that should keep it under control." As she saw the very concerned look on my face, she added, "I'll be okay, Matt. Please relax and smile for me. It's what I need right now."

I had not realized how serious my expression had been and quickly smiled while telling her, "I'm sure the doctors are right. This should not be a problem, and I really look forward to seeing you back at your home this evening." I held her hand for a moment and gave her a huge smile.

While leaving the room, she said, "God bless you for being such a good neighbor."

Hearing the door to her room close behind me brought me back into Johns Hopkins again—this time I was encompassed with fear. Doing an assessment of my situation helped me gain control of the PTSD, something I learned in my training as a counselor. The question that had to be answered at the moment was, "Where are you physically right now?" My inner being answered, *Visiting Sara in her hospital.* Then thoughts came of how God had carried me through my darkest days of surgery and I remembered about never being alone. This prevented the fear from overtaking my ability to function. Leaving the hospital made everything even easier as it had done in the past. Walking out the front door brought me back in the parking lot of the local hospital.

Sara was discharged at the end of the day, and I was relieved that Trish, a retired teacher and church member, had brought her home. Upon arrival, Sara called to ask me to come over and explain to Trish what happened and how she could help. I recommended Trish stay with Sara overnight and to call me if anything happened. Trish was curious about my ability to help and was relieved after learning some of my background, experience, and availability. She felt even better that what Sara was going through did not require immediate emergency attention and was assured that everything would be all right. Sara's face lit up with a smile as she knew how much people cared for her, and with Trish staying at her house, she would not have to face a seizure alone if she were to have one.

The doctors at the local hospital realized something very serious was occurring with Sara and made arrangements for her to see a stroke neurologist at the VCU Epilepsy Center about a hundred miles away. They may have explained this to Sara before she left, but at the time, they didn't realize the severity of her inability to remember what she was told. The part of her brain that was under siege did not impact her cognitive abilities, but it did impact her long-term memory. Fortunately, they had put the appointment down in writing, and Trish had seen the discharge papers. She told both of us about the appointment and asked if she could help. Sara appreciated and accepted her offer. The appointment with a neurologist specializing in strokes was a couple of weeks away. I made a mental note of Trish's offer and willingness to help.

More challenges would befall us as time progressed. It turned out that the fires of the hell were being stoked once again.

Chapter 12

It started to rain the day Sara came home and it rained for the next several days. Her seizure and my response were the start of a very close relationship. On such miserable days, most of my time was spent setting up the wood shop in the shed in the backyard. It was like a safe haven. Sara was curious about my ability to recognize her seizures and that I knew what to do so, she came over and let herself in. Imagine my surprise when I looked up from the lathe and someone was standing in front of me, watching.

"Oh. Hi, Sara."

"Hi, Matt. Sorry I surprised you, but it was interesting watching you turn that piece of wood into a beautiful shape. We haven't seen each other for a few days, and I've been wondering how you knew what to do when I came over for help the other night. You asked some very appropriate questions that I would never have thought to ask the doctor."

"I've been living with epilepsy for many years and have been a mentor and counselor for people and families struggling with the unknowns of seizures. I've had similar experiences and seeing your eyes and you telling me of the replay of your dog fetching the ball made it easy for me to recognize your seizure." I didn't tell her that I was thinking of her while unknowingly, she was standing right in front of me.

We looked at each other for a few moments, just smiling at each other. She then said, "You told me you had brain surgery, but I'd like to know more of the details about how you survived the seizures. Based on the hospital report received today, it looks like you may be a great source for me to learn to live with mine. How about coming over for dinner tonight so we can talk? And not just about epilepsy."

She had a beaming smile that melted my heart; all I could say was "That would be nice."

She responded, "Great. See you at six-thirty," as she walked out of the shop.

That evening, she made a scrumptious meal of steak on the grill, fresh vegetables, and a salad. Dessert was my favorite, a blueberry pie topped with vanilla ice cream. She was surprised as I helped her clean up the kitchen, and we settled down on the sofa to talk. Apparently, the men she had known never did such a thing. With a full stomach of my favorite foods, I gave her my total attention and let her know I was ready to listen. She was hoping to learn about what to expect with recovery through my experience with brain surgery as she was having some difficulty getting her thoughts together to get organized at home and at work.

As her eyes locked with mine, she told me more about her stroke and recovery. Her tone and mannerism were reminiscent of that of a pastor talking in church, which was maybe her way of dealing with the trauma of what she lived through. "My stroke occurred about six months ago while I was the pastor of another church. It was my first time being the senior pastor and I was working through a learning curve as the various Christian holidays came along. Christmas was the hardest as it was my first time working with the congregation during the very busy holiday season. I was stressed and forgot to delegate some of the responsibilities to the staff and volunteers."

Knowing how stress was a key trigger to seizures, I was very interested to learn how it had affected her. She was describing to me a significant increase in workload along with the emotional stress of being accepted by the congregation.

She continued, "To make matters worse, it was a couple of weeks before Christmas, and I was very busy with church events, special services, and extra work with the congregation. It was early in the morning as I walked into the church and suddenly had a tremendously agonizing headache. The pain dropped me to my knees, and I could barely move. I was able to get my cell phone out of my purse and press the emergency number for my secretary. My memory of all this is vivid. All the details will never be lost. Maggie answered her phone and seeing my number immediately told me she was fifteen minutes away as she was commuting to the church. I remember what I tried to say, but Maggie later told me she could not understand my garbled words but recognized my phone number and the panicky tone of my voice. She then told me she was putting me on hold and calling 911. This should have brought me relief, but the pain in my head was like nothing I'd ever experienced before. It literally felt like my head was going to explode. I thought Maggie had hung up because it seemed to take forever before I heard her voice again. She said she was within a few minutes of the church, and the emergency medical technicians (EMT) were already there, searching for me. We were fortunate the fire station was just across the street." As I listened, it seemed Maggie's quick reaction was the first part of the miracle that saved Sara.

Sara then talked of being found stricken in the hallway near her office. The EMTs recognized her stroke symptoms and raced her to the hospital. As the ambulance pulled in, there was a special team of doctors and technicians waiting at the door who went to work on her before she was even completely inside the building.

She then became quiet for a moment, like she was intensely recalling that part of the experience. She then continued, "Maggie's reaction was wonderful because while the EMTs and stroke team were working on me, she contacted my husband right away, then several people within the church, and Emily, my niece. She then called the district office, and they had another pastor rush to the hospital where they gave me the last rites to prepare my soul to leave, as my body was failing, by blessing me with grace through anointment and prayer. Hearing this brought me into the reality of the situation. Everyone thought my life was over, except a doctor who wouldn't quit, and me.

"I was not expected to live because the damage to my brain was significant, but my body was in good shape from running and I was able to fight back. Emily arrived as soon as she could get on an airline and spent all her time in the hospital's intensive care unit (ICU) with me. My whole left side was paralyzed, including half my face, and the pain was so intense it crippled my entire body. It would take several days before everything slowed down and my recovery started. I was never going to give up and I really wanted to be in church as soon as possible for a Sunday service. Within a couple of weeks, Emily and several parishioners were able to make arrangements with several members of the church to take me to a service."

Sara was a fighter like me. She explained how she had been running in marathons, which helped immensely in her recovery, so her body was actually in tremendous shape and able to take the shock of the stroke. I recognized how her brain began to rewire as she explained her creating a demand to stimulate the nerves, even though it took many days of working with physical trainers. The functioning nerves rewired through different pathways, and her ability to use her left arm and leg returned within a month. I knew her ability to feel what she touched would take several years through a friend who was in an accident and was paralyzed from the waist down for a while; their nerves recovered a couple inches per month, and years later, no one could even tell that they had ever had such an injury. Sara was another example as she talked of how it took several weeks for the muscles in her face to function normally again and she could fully smile once more; maybe that explained why her smile radiated all the time. Three months after her stroke, she had returned to work.

I grinned at her and thanked her for sharing, then told her she should feel blessed. "You are a walking miracle. Very few people who have strokes that bleed like yours survive, let alone are able to recover and function so well. I am blessed in meeting you."

She smiled for a moment, then looked sad as she explained how her time away from the church and the unknowns of her ability to continue as the pastor-in-charge led to her replacement. The regional office worked with her through her recovery and helped by finding part-time work until she could be reassigned. The outcome led to us becoming neighbors. She had been dealing with the stress and struggles of finding a new home, relating to a different congregation, and starting over with becoming established in the community several hundred miles from where she used to work.

Hearing the word *stress* made me wonder if this was the cause of her recent seizure. So, I asked, "Sara, was this the first time you had any odd feelings or jerking movement?"

She gave me a questioning look and then seemed to think about it for a moment. "No, my left arm used to jerk a little, and I got a twitching in my face."

"Did the doctors ever tell you anything about the possibility of having a seizure while in recovery?"

"No, they never mentioned it."

"When did the twitching occur, and how often? Have you ever lost consciousness?"

"Just before moving here, I was with a friend when my arm started to jerk, and they said my face looked weird. I felt fine within a minute or so."

I began to wonder if the seizures had been occurring in her brain for quite some time but had just not affected her cognitive abilities. My experience and research led me to know how this can occur for many months where the seizures are local, affecting only a small part of the brain, then break through to other areas that control a person's physical abilities. Such breakthroughs can become more and more intense if not treated, eventually affecting the entire brain. Had the doctors told her about the potential for seizures or ever tested for them?

My face must have had a very serious expression as she went quiet and watched me closely, then asked, "What are you thinking about?"

"I'm wondering how long you have been having seizure-like symptoms."

It seemed it was time to share some of my experience, the impact to my family, and my struggles with seizures and surgery. I shared how it impacted my marriage when the seizures became intractable, and there seemed to be no hope of my gaining control. It was not until going to one of the top epilepsy research hospitals, where they discovered the source of the seizures in my brain, that hope returned.

Her mouth dropped open as she listened to how surgery involved removal of a section of my left temporal lobe to allow access to the source of the seizures, my left hippocampus. I finished by saying, "Now you understand my ability to relate to what happened to you with the stroke."

Her mouth closed, with a look of amazement on her face. As she listened, Sara saw a man who had been living with the fear of seizures since he was a child, then struggling with the stigma of epilepsy for more than fifty years. Now with her seizure, she was more amazed with my ability to not only survive but to live a full life, even after having brain surgery. She seemed to relax as she realized my inimitable ability to associate with some of the trauma she had experienced.

I told her how no one knew what the surgery's final outcome would be. Would I know who I was? Would my short-term memory be damaged? Would I be able to remember my family and children? Knowing she was a pastor, I added, "Would my soul be cut away?" In order to inspire her, I said, "I was terrified yet had a faith that everything would come through. Significant memory issues ensued yet my being determined helped with the recovery. It would take several years, and part of it was possible by my being the person in need. This enabled other people to answer a calling in their faith to be the provider. My wife loved me dearly and we were married for over twenty-five years, but the stress she experienced with the surgery, then being my caregiver that eventually led to our divorce. I'm not angry at her, only frustrated that it happened this way."

Sara realized that the trauma of my seizures and surgery with the impact to friends and family was as devastating as her stroke. She said, "My husband could not help me when my stroke occurred. I guess he thought I was going to die and could not take it." She looked very sad and went quiet for a while. Bouts of countertransference hit me as I listened to the many similarities to my own experience.

I must have had a look of regret, so she continued, rubbing her hands together in nervousness. "The last time I saw him was the morning of the stroke. He gave me a hug and told me to have a good day as he hurried out of the house and got into his car. When he got the call from Maggie, he refused to come to the hospital. He just turned his phone off. I haven't seen or heard from him since, except for appearing in court for the divorce. He said nothing to me even then and kept looking away." A whiff of apprehension shot through me triggered by the similarities in our injuries and struggles to survive.

She went on to explain how she had to battle to recover from the stroke on her own as she had no one living with her yet was dependent on many for transportation and basic assistance. After weeks of being in the hospital and in a rehabilitation center where she learned to walk and use her arm again, she was allowed to go home. That's when she realized what it would be like to live alone. Her husband had left and none of the bills that were due each month had been paid. The shock of the whole situation with the stroke, the resulting disabilities, and the abandonment by her husband immobilized her ability to function at home and as a leader at her church. Now I understood the reason the church had to replace her at the time. They needed to provide for the congregation. Her world had been turned upside down in just a moment. Recovery both physically and emotionally required time, with the outcome being unknown. Silence filled the room again as she looked down, appearing to have relived the worst scenario imagined, yet it had actually happened.

I felt sorry for her and eventually broke the silence, "I'm so sorry to hear what you have been through. Once more, I'm a witness to a miracle with your ability to keep moving and now being a pastor again. Keeping a positive attitude is part of God's plan, and there is always meaning to our lives."

She looked at me with a gentle smile and said, "Matt, you're a good man and what I need right now is to get reestablished." This was something she would regularly say as she could read me through her own experience. It was a reminder of who I was.

A strong sense of fear and loss came over me while giving her a goodbye hug that night, making me wonder, *Why at this time?* As I left the house, my environment changed, and the anxiety subsided. An aura never came.

The rain that had been coming down for most of the day ceased just as I walked away from her house. My emotions were calmed with the change in environment, enabling me to think about our current roles as a pastor and counselor and how our similarities could be good for the community. It seemed that we should be working together, but why did the sense of fear hit me so hard?

My struggle to understand my role with Sara led me to my backyard and praying over what was happening. My conscience was telling me to only be a mentor, and my soul was saying there was a special role for me to fulfill. Suddenly, everything around me was enveloped in a soothing blue light as a full moon shone. It was truly amazing to watch how the moon remained visible as the clouds of the massive storm swirled around it.

The light of moon was protected by a special pocket that caused any cloud that should have blanked it out to split apart, allowing the rays of the moon to shine down and light up the darkness I felt enveloped in. A feeling of God's presence came across me while watching this phenomenon, and any tension and fear of Sara faded away from me. I kept watching the sky as the clouds split around the moon and the light kept coming through. This seemed to go on for a long time, but eventually, the clouds won over and the rain came pouring down again. It seemed that God put me and Sara close together so we could help each other recover from the storms we had faced and to eventually work together, or so I thought.

Sara was surprised a few days later when I came over to check on her. Her stroke and its outcome had scared many people, and she feared it had driven me away too. I shared my experience of being in the backyard and praying while witnessing the storm and the moon. We agreed it would be good to see each other a few evenings later to talk about our roles in being neighbors and helping each other.

We both were feeling a strong pull toward working together. Time away enabled us to process what had been happening in our lives and our being neighbors. When the time came for us to talk about our situation and feelings, our conclusions were similar. We both felt a stronger power coming from God that brought us together. Through her training and work as a social worker, pastor, and stroke survivor, Sara saw the weakness in me caused by the mental challenges associated with brain surgery and the fear of living with epilepsy for so long. She wanted me to feel whole and be a man who was proud of himself. I would be her mentor, helping her with recovery from the stroke and to help her understand her ability to be independent. What we didn't realize was how our caring for each other led to a loving nurture neither of us had ever experienced before.

Chapter 13

Our dinners together seemed to be occurring more regularly, as eating with two people was much more fun than eating alone. She shared many stories about sailing and living on boats and listened to some of mine about sailing on smaller classes of boats and backpacking in the mountains. We were always so excited to have some time together.

One night, I came into her kitchen to help finish making dinner and noticed she was unstable, and her left arm was trembling. When we sat down, she started to tell me more about what was troubling her. "Matt, you told me about the difficulty you had with math after your surgery. Please share with me how you recovered. I'm having much difficulty paying bills and can't keep track of my accounts."

"What do you find so difficult?"

"I can't process numbers."

To better understand the situation, I thought of what my neurologist asked me the day after my surgery and said, "What's a hundred minus seven?"

She got a serious look on her face as she tried to process the numbers in her mind.

"I don't know!"

It made me uncomfortable to remember what it had been like for me. She noticed me shifting in the chair and sitting up straighter. Hoping she, at least, understood the fundamentals, I asked, "Which is bigger, a hundred or a thousand?"

"I know that a thousand is larger but cannot comprehend by how much," she said.

Without thinking, I responded, "A thousand is ten times larger than a hundred."

She looked down for a moment as she was trying to grasp what I said. She then looked up and told me, "I recognize the multiplication but still cannot comprehend the value or magnitude of the numbers. What happens when something is multiplied by ten?"

I smiled at her and said, "Let's count how many fingers you have."

"I have ten."

I then replied, "How do you know? You didn't count them. Let's count and see how many you really have."

Without pause, she pointed to each finger and counted. "One … Two … Three … Four … Five … Six … Seven … Eight … Nine … Ten. I have ten fingers."

"Now imagine each of your fingers is one of you. How many of you does all your fingers represent?"

"Ten."

"Can you count by ten?"

She paused for a moment, and her eyes looked away from me. Then she looked right at me and pointed to each finger as she said, "Ten. Twenty. Thirty. Forty. Fifty. Sixty. Seventy. Eighty. Ninety. A hundred." A huge smile came over her face as she finished.

I then said, "So ten of you would have one hundred fingers. I must confess though, I'm glad there is only one of you!"

Her smile became a giant grin as she started to laugh. Her laugh brought a smile back to my face as the door closed on the vision in my head that had me in a bed at Johns Hopkins, being asked by my doctor again and again, "What's a hundred minus seven, minus seven …"

"Looks like we will have to work on getting your brain to adjust so you can comprehend and do math again. It is going to take some time and effort, but you'll recover," I said.

With a wavering smile, she asked, "How are you so sure?"

"Because I've been there. You see, the function of the part of the brain they took out of me is like the RAM in a computer.[*] It processes information coming in and retrieves information stored in the front of the brain. Most of one of mine was removed. Recovery requires reprogramming the brain, which happens when there is a need to do so. You'll reach points along the way that will keep you motivated." Looking straight into her eyes, I added with a smile, "Prayer is a tremendous help. You have to believe."

She smiled back. "Thank you for sharing and the reminder. What you said makes sense of my experience. I couldn't remember much of what I'd read for several months after the stroke. I would read all morning and couldn't remember anything about it, not even the name of the book. It has gotten much better, especially reading a book I've read before. It seems to open up my memory. Does this mean I'm reprograming?"

She made me chuckle. My engineering thought process had come out again in my manner of explaining everything. "Yes, the brain is like a muscle. If you don't use it, it won't improve. Seems you already know some of this through your reading comprehension and experience as a runner in preparing for a marathon."

Mentioning this seemed to bring her a sense of relief as the tension lines faded from her face. Her growing smile seemed very real.

To meet another person who could relate so well to brain injury inspired a sense of peace and security both of us never experienced before. It was a peace that included feelings that divine intervention brought us together because we could understand each other without question. The common injuries and traumas we shared brought us security. Now both of us struggled to fully rebound from our brain injuries. Our positive attitudes and refusal to quit provided an instant and continuing bond. We laughed together as we realized we now had a whole brain between us: her left side and my right.

---

[*]RAM is the random-access memory

Chapter 14

Everything in our relationship was happening suddenly. We had known each other for several months yet felt like we'd known one another for many years. I thought it would be good for her to see another part of me and test her ability to get up in the wee hours of the morning to go fishing.

I invited her to join me to go fishing or, if nothing else, see the sunrise. She was excited about being able to demonstrate her love of being on the water, then winced when I told her, "I'll be leaving at four-thirty tomorrow morning." She promised to be there and asked if she could make breakfast. She told me about her breakfast burrito and inquired what I'd like on it. My response, "No coffee and just the basics: an egg and bacon on the burrito, please." She smiled and said she would add a few ingredients to make it a true burrito and something she was sure to wake me up. At the moment, I was feeling that the probability of her joining me was slim to none and told her, "I'll wait for you, but I plan to leave on time."

The next morning, I was up early and had a light breakfast before heading out because I was certain Sara would not be joining me. She just didn't seem to be a morning person. The truck, boat, and tackle were ready to go, but Sara still had five minutes. I went out in front of her house to see if any additional lighting was on but did not see anything different as she typically left the kitchen light on throughout the night. I just knew she was not coming yet waited as promised.

With one-minute left, she came out of her front door and walked toward my truck. I was glad I didn't bet money on the probability of her joining me as it would have cost me a fortune. As she climbed into the truck, she leaned over and gave me a kiss on the cheek. I felt myself blush in the face and it made me appreciate how dark it was that morning as it wouldn't be as noticeable. As we drove to the boat ramp, she handed me a very hot burrito and said, "Here's the breakfast I promised." The fact that she was up way before I was, then to have gotten dressed and cooked such a scrumptious breakfast demonstrated a love that must be true. The burrito was delicious! Just as she promised, she had spiced it enough to make it hot, and I was wide awake with the first bite as my senses were overwhelmed by Tabasco sauce. They say, "The way to a man's heart is through his stomach," and she was right on the mark.

It was a thirty-minute ride to the ramp, and we felt we were in heaven the whole way. We got the boat in the water, and Sara looked great sitting beside me as we motored along the waterway to the main river. I rigged a rod for her and taught her how to cast, something she had to relearn as her stroke still impacted her ability to coordinate the use of her left hand. She asked, "How can you be so calm and understanding of my disabilities?"

"A friend of mine at work lost the use of his left hand in a bicycle accident. He told me how sad it made him to see his stand-up bass instrument in the corner of his room and not be able to play because he could not hold a bow. I made him a glove that the bow would attach to, and he is playing his bass again. It is the importance of having a mind-set to live with the disability that enables one to overcome it," I replied.

"Are you still friends?"

"Oh yes! He showed the glove to his doctor, and she had one made by a professional that fits even better. I hear from him occasionally online. He actually played in a concert with his son again."

As she looked at me, there was a twinkle in her eyes, and her smile broadened as she realized how much she was being cared for.

We fished for several hours, and eventually she looked very tired. We reached our limit and headed back to the ramp. It was nice to have her along, and I could not wait until the next time we would go fishing. When we got home, she told me how getting up so early left her feeling exhausted, and she went back to her house. I cleaned up the boat and filleted the fish, looking forward to having dinner with her that evening.

Her desire to be on the water demonstrated her will to get better. She wanted to be able to go back to what she enjoyed. We both loved the water and would spend many a morning fishing in the early dawn. Each time, she needed less and less help and caught more fish. In fact, her disability in her hand gave her an advantage as it provided a motion that made the lure appear as a wounded fish; this attracted many of the big fish, and she cheered as she reeled them in.

Chapter 15

As Sara was getting established in her church and learned of my experience working with teams of people and individuals as a manager and counselor, she started to develop a plan for us to work together. She would work with the congregation, and I would work with the people, focusing initially on the men. To demonstrate the seriousness of the proposal, she invited me over for dinner. This time, she had her dining room table set. Seeing her notebook placed beside her sitting area made me realize this was going to be a work session.

She smiled when she heard my stomach growl, knowing she now had my undivided attention as we sat down to eat another of her wonderful meals. We were about to start eating when she opened her notebook and started telling me about her plan.

"I've come up with an idea and I need your input on how to implement it. You see, I want to get the men more involved at the church and would love to hear your ideas. You need to know that the notes keep me from forgetting what we talk about, so be careful what you say." She gave me a big grin, wanting me to know that she was implementing one of my suggestions to help with her memory and was so excited to get started. I sat at the table politely listening as our food was getting cold. It was difficult to listen, as I was distracted by the wonderful aroma of the food. It made my mouth water.

"There are not many men participating in the church, and I would like you to become one of the leaders of the Sunday school and be a speaker once in a while. I need you to set an example and apply your pastoral counseling skills. Would you be interested in doing something like this?" She already knew the answer and gave me a beaming smile to assure I couldn't refuse. Before I could say anything, my stomach growled again, and she heard it.

I responded with, "Only if you say grace and let me start eating your awesome dinner." Then I gave her a smile I knew she couldn't resist.

She laughed. "I'm so sorry. I didn't mean to torment you into agreeing. So, you agree this would be good?"

"I'm not sure. My stomach has control of my thought process right now, so it may take a while before I'm able to give you an honest answer."

She bowed her head as she said, "Heavenly Father, we give you thanks for this food and the opportunities you bless us with through our work in sharing your Word. Amen!"

I said "Amen," then picked up my fork and began eating; in a short period of time my stomach was content, and I could start thinking more clearly about her idea. "I don't think just participating in the church would be sufficient. What about expanding your idea into setting up a men's ministry in the community? It would be a men's group that would meet on a weekday morning or evening someplace other than the church," I suggested.

I caught her with her mouth full and had to wait a minute as she quickly chewed her food. There was excitement all over her face as she waited to speak. I already knew what she was going to say as she wrote in her notebook.

"I think that would be wonderful! I'll need you to hold off a little while until I get better situated in the church and community. You know we are only friends, and I don't want people to think you are the person in charge of the church, especially with how many people believe about the roles of men and women. Their bias may have them believe I am the assistant pastor."

For a moment, a sense of uneasiness came over me triggered by memories of talking to many different people who shared their biases about the roles of women in the church. What made me so interested and willing to work with Sara was that she wanted to take on the challenge to overcome such bias and set the record straight on a woman's ability to be a leader. It made me believe even more that God had brought us together as our work would enable the church to reach out to everyone in the community.

We were both very excited because our togetherness went far beyond ourselves as we discussed the details of our upcoming ministries. The next thing we knew, it was nearly midnight, and the dirty dishes were still on the table. She looked very tired. Seeing her left-hand twitching, I told her, "You need to get some sleep. Why don't you get ready for bed, and I'll take care of cleaning up the dishes and the kitchen?"

As she was leaving the room, she said, "I'm sorry we didn't get to eat dessert tonight. I made you another pie and had ice cream to go with it."

I jokingly gave her a look of disappointment, then shrugged my shoulders as I said, "Well, I'll just have to come back tomorrow evening."

She gave me that huge smile again as she hugged me and gave me a kiss on the cheek. As she pulled away, she squeezed my hand, then had to leave the room to take care of herself.

I let Samuel outside, then cleaned up the kitchen. I thought Sara's plan was very good and I was excited about how she wanted me to be a part of her future in the ministry. After letting Samuel back in, there came a rhythmic sound from Sara's room; she was asleep, but her arm was jerking. It continued for only a few seconds, and then all seemed well. The future seemed so bright, and through our plans, it seemed that God must have truly brought us together to do His work.

Chapter 16

Sara visited my house a few times a week as we worked on the details of her plan of us working together in the community. Our friendship continued to develop, and we shared more of our past and ability to associate so easily with each other. We challenged each other with mental drills. For me, the challenge was names; for her, it was math. Neither of us became frustrated because we understood each other's disability and could laugh about it together. She enjoyed the porch on my house with its three sides of windows and loved the layout of the kitchen. Seeing no furniture in my living room, she offered to give me a table, couch, and lazy back chair she had stored in a bedroom at her house. She appreciated that I accepted the offer because now she had a usable bedroom for guests, and I had a furnished living room where we could meet. We would later learn the importance of having such furniture in my house in helping with her disability.

Throughout this time, her seizures were occurring a few times a week but had remained simple, and we were able to enjoy the outdoors without any worry of either of us losing consciousness. This all seemed to bring us a better understanding of each other through the respect we both shared of a simple type of seizure. A couple of times I had auras that no one noticed except Sara. She now had an insight that enabled her to recognize these when no one else could, and she showed a caring for me by holding my hand the few times it happened.

The best time to be outside in the summer was in the early morning or late evening as it became too hot and humid during the middle of the day. Fishing in the morning and going for walks in the evening a few days a week became our routine. We had no contact on Saturdays because that was when she needed time to write her sermons and get ready for the Sunday services.

Our relationship continued to develop as we spent more time together. We shared dinner often as we discovered a harmony neither had ever felt before, with a sense of special caring enhanced by our life experiences. This would continue for a short while until brought to a halt by what we feared the most.

It was a Sunday morning, and Sara was to be at the church soon to lead the service. I was getting ready to go to my church when she called and in a panicky voice cried, "Can you help me? I cannot get dressed, and I'm late for the service!"

I ran next door and this time did not knock, simply jerked opened the door and ran inside. My fear was intensifying, fed by thoughts of finding Sara on the floor having a seizure. Instead, she was in her kitchen; part of her blouse was unbuttoned, and her clerical collar was sitting on the counter. She could not finish buttoning her blouse because her left hand was twitching, and she had no control of it. I immediately recognized she was having a simple partial seizure and on the verge of a panic attack.

Sara was so distressed because she needed to get to the church soon to be able to lead the early service; she had no one to take her place and, being the pastor for less than a year, was terrified what the congregation would think of her if she was late. I finished buttoning her blouse, and she explained how to attach the collar as I worked to get it on her. Seeing her arm jerk caused feelings of dread to run through me. It was important for me to keep a calm disposition to ease the situation while telling her "Everything will work out, and you will do very well. You're a great pastor, and your message will far outweigh being a few minutes late. I'll take good care of Samuel. Now get on your way."

She gave me that quick kiss on the cheek and then rushed out the door, jumped in her car, and sped down the street. Even

Samuel felt relief from the stress of the situation now that she was gone, and he looked at me and wagged his tail.

It was Monday afternoon when I saw Sara again as she was in her backyard, playing with Samuel. She looked tired, and we talked about how her two services had gone.

"I could not believe how my arm was shaking as I drove to the church. I hope no one saw it twitching during the service."

"How did you do during the service?" I asked.

"I did fine actually. Except my arm twitched once in a while. I am afraid people will see my arm or leg jerking and reject me from the church. There are some people in the church who want to get rid of me because they do not like female pastors."

"So how did you get home yesterday? I thought I'd seen another vehicle in the driveway," I replied.

"My arm started twitching constantly after the service, and my vision was somewhat impaired. So, I thought it best to get a ride home. A couple quickly volunteered to drive for me and brought my car home too."

I smiled and joked, "Ah, so there are some good Christians at your church after all! Tell me, have you been taking your medication? If you miss a dose, you could have a seizure." Sara gave me a very serious look, so I followed with, "Driving was a key stressor for my seizures and seems to be for yours too. Next week, I'll change my denomination and start coming to your church. That way, you do not have to worry about transportation, and you can concentrate on what you love to do: preach! With time, you should get control of this and will no longer need my help."

Her face filled with joy and relief overcame her worries now that she knew someone would make sure she was safe. She gave me a big hug to thank me for answering her silent cry for help. That night, we went for a walk down near the water. She wanted to hold my hand as she gave me that wonderful smile and said, "We are meant to be with each other." Her hand had a special warmth as she tightly held onto mine.

When it came time to go home, she gave me a big hug. I held her tight, neither of us wanting to let go. It was a way to express our faith that things would get better. Indeed, we were meant for each other as the traumas of the past and present were coming together. Neither of us realized we were on the edge of an intense storm. Her complex partial seizures would start ten days later.

I stopped to think about what I just said, then realized what time it was and knew this was a good place to finish the session for the day. I motioned to Carol that I was done and that we needed the lights in the room turned up. It seemed like this story would have a happy ending, but I already knew the outcome brought on sadness. This was one of those times I wished this was a story that I had made up instead of actually lived.

As the lights became brighter, Carol came out to tell everyone, "This case gets even more interesting, so be sure to be back on Wednesday morning at ten o'clock." I then walked over to Carol to let her know I'd be back at nine-thirty the next day, as she seemed a little nervous about my continuing the talk. She smiled and told me that the doors would be unlocked and looked forward to seeing me again.

A sense of relief came over me as I headed to the entrance to the building and knowing that being outside in the warmth and sunshine always helped to reenergize me. Near one side of the entrance sat Helen, waiting for Mark to bring the car over. She was waving at me, and then shouted to get my attention, as my mind was in another place. I managed to smile and walked over to her.

"Tell me more about how Sara recovered so fast," she said. The answer I had was easy. "Determination," I said. "She believed her mission as a pastor was not over and as a fighter she was determined to continue in that role. The mind will rewire itself if there is a need to do so."

Then I asked, "What will it take to get you so determined that you would work harder in your recovery?" She quickly answered, "Sara's story. Thank you, I will never forget what you said today. God bless you for sharing your story."

My smile broadened and I became more motivated and inspired. "God bless you too Helen. I look forward to meeting you again someday and hearing your story." I gave her a hug and stayed until Mark arrived.

Section III

The Mentor

Wednesday, day three, was a chance to share what it was like for me to be a mentor to someone. As I sat in the back of the room, watching the people come in, and listened to their conversations, I was assured that many could relate through similar experiences. It was a young boy who caught my attention the most that morning. He was sitting with his mother right in front of me. I had noticed as they came up to their seats that they both had very serious expressions on their faces, like they had heard the worst kind of news. As I got up from my seat to join Carol the boy's arm jerked suddenly several times, and he appeared to be staring off to the left, typical of an absence seizure. His mother put her arm around him and kissed him on top of his head. Tears started forming in my eyes as I walked down the stairs.

Once again, Carol started the meeting and introduced me as I walked out to the podium. As people saw me look at them, several smiled and waved at me, waiting to hear what I had to say. Seeing the mother and her son gave me the motivation I needed to continue. I stood quietly, waiting for several people who were still chatting to be respectful and become quiet. It did not take more than a minute until the room was totally silent.

My training as a counselor and assessing situations kicked in as I looked at the audience and saw everyone quietly looking down at me. Something about the boy and his mother in the audience reminded me of the importance of talking about the role of a mentor, perchance engraining a sense of hope in them. It was time to continue.

Chapter 17

It was now early Fall, and as promised, I had changed over from my church to attending Sara's and being her mode of transportation and mentor during the services. She had been doing very well with no major issues with her seizures since she didn't have to worry about driving. I arrived early at her house and was relieved once again that she had control of her left arm and was completely dressed. She said she felt good and was excited about having control of her body. We actually laughed with each other because having seizures was something we both could relate to, and laughter was our manner of burying fear. We arrived at the church early, and she gave me a huge smile and a quick hug as she went to get her vestment from her office. I headed to the sanctuary and was welcomed and felt comfortable sitting with the members of the congregation.

It was wonderful to see her in action as the pastor as she led the first service and delivered her sermon. The following service came two hours later, and we had Sunday school in between. Once again, she seemed comfortable and interacted with everyone. We talked for a few minutes before the second service started, and she appeared nervous as her smile disappeared.

I asked, "How are you doing? Thought I saw your arm jerk a few times."

She had a look of concern in the seriousness of her expression. "I don't know what is happening. I am feeling very nervous for some reason. I've done this several times now and even for larger congregations, so why am I so nervous now?" she said.

I recognized these symptoms as a simple type of seizure but didn't say anything about it. "I'll be up front in the congregation this time and can come forward and help you if needed. I can assure the congregation you will be all right if something happens. Don't get caught up worrying about your seizures. You are in good hands," I assured and pointed toward the cross on the wall. She told me that this brought some comfort knowing I was available to take over if she felt something developing with her seizures. This time, I gave her a great, big hug, then headed for the chapel.

The service went well, with the exception of the blessing of the collection of the congregation's financial gifts. As she went to raise the collection plate for the blessing, it slipped from her left hand. She had not raised it far above the table when this happened, and I thought no one noticed since nothing spilled. She recovered quickly, leaving it on the table as she said the blessing. Her arm continued to jerk for a few minutes, however, she did well with the rest of the service, except she was not singing with everyone during the closing hymn.

Soon after performing the blessing of the congregation, she slipped out the back of the chapel using the shortcut to her office. When I found her, she was close to tears as she struggled with unzipping her vestment. Upon my entering the room, she looked up and let go of her robe, shouting, "I can't even undo a zipper, let alone handle a collection plate!" She was having a partial seizure and had lost the use of her left arm.

I forced a smile and said, "If you had not told me, I would have never known what happened. By the way, it appears the problem is that your zipper is stuck. Let me fix it." I helped get her robe off, placed it on the oversize hanger, and hung it up in her closet. She seemed much calmer, and her arm stopped jerking. She looked pale, and it seemed that all she wanted to do was go home. Before leaving I asked, "Does any part of your body feel out of control?"

She seemed much calmer as she responded, "I am fine now, I just wanna go home. You'll drive, won't you?"

I was relieved knowing her seizure was over and said, "Can do," as she handed me her car keys.

As we rode home, she talked of the emotional struggle she was having when she felt the loss of control of her hand and dropped the collection plate. "I was about to cry, then remembered you were sitting in the front pew. It brought me a sense of peace knowing how you remain calm and could help me and the congregation if the seizure were to progress."

She placed her left hand on mine, and it made me feel good that I helped calm the turmoil she faced. I was thinking about my role of caring for her and what to do to keep the congregation safe from the fear of her having a seizure. We smiled at each other, then her arm jerked, and the reality of the situation returned. I kept smiling, but with a sense of loss racing through my mind as her smile was replaced by an expression of deep concern, and she pulled her hand from mine.

By the time we arrived home, she had lost control of her left arm as it was jerking continuously. She made it into her house and collapsed on the couch. The left side of her body was out of control, jerking arithmetically. Her seizure was now in the full ictal stage. She was conscious of what was happening and cried out "Please make it stop!" over and over again. I checked the time and managed to get a video of what was happening while calmly assuring her that she would be okay. This phase of the seizure lasted for two and a half minutes, well within the five-minute limit. She was exhausted, so I got her a blanket and pillow to help make her comfortable.

While she slept, I called Trish to see if she could stay with her for several days until she could see the stroke neurologist. The appointment was two weeks away, but with the seizure that occurred, we hoped it could be moved up to within the next day or so. Trish was an angel who came and helped. What had happened left me rather distressed, and recovery required me to have some time away from the area. It was around dinner time when Sara woke up. She looked much better, was showing no signs of any seizure activity, and had complete control of her arm. Trish informed me of Sara's status and asked me to come over to help make dinner.

That night, we spent some time together to talk about what Sara had experienced with her seizure and the importance of seeing her neurologist. She seemed overwhelmed, nearly in tears as she told me, "I got a phone call this afternoon from a member of the congregation. They saw what happened and told me I was possessed and that they were leaving the church." This was a topic I had not shared with Sara; she had enough going on with the battle she was fighting to recover from her stroke and now the seizures. That so many people to this day still consider us possessed was tragic, and I couldn't imagine what it would do to someone like Sara at her weakest moment.

I got her Bible off the table and opened it to Matthew 17. "This was read to me a month after my surgery. I was in a meeting at the church I attended with several other people and the pastor started by reading this scripture. That pastor turned pale when she finished reading because she saw me in the second part of it, as if she had read my story. She didn't realize what an uplift it was for me. "I hope the same holds true for you," I said as I gave her a smile, then started reading.

> Six days later, Jesus took with him Peter and James and his brother John and led them up a high mountain, by themselves. And he was transfigured before them, and his face shone like the sun, and his clothes became dazzling white.

Sara looked at me and said, "I know this scripture very well, we do a sermon based on it every year."

"Then you know that the rest of this part is about the transfiguration of Jesus. Let me skip ahead a little to when they first come off the mountain and read the part that applies to us," I continued.

> When they came to the crowd, a man came to him, knelt before him, and said, "Lord, have mercy on my son, for he is an epileptic and he suffers terribly; he often falls into the fire and often into the water. And I brought him to your disciples, but they could not cure him." Jesus answered, "You faithless and perverse generation, how much longer must I be with you? How much longer must I put up with you? Bring him here to me." And Jesus rebuked the demon, and it came out of him, and the boy was cured instantly. Then the disciples came to Jesus privately and said, "Why could we not cast it out?" He said to them, "Because of your little faith. For truly I tell you, if you have faith the size of a mustard seed, you will say to this mountain, 'Move from here to there,' and it will move; and nothing will be impossible for you."

I looked up at her, and she was staring at the Bible, deep in thought. I waited a moment, then said, "The child going into the fire and the water were his attempts of suicide, caused by how he was treated and isolated because people feared his seizures. This fear led to the persecution of people with epilepsy through exorcism, drowning, and burning for hundreds of years. When that stopped, we were sterilized through the 1950's, and marriage was outlawed for us until 1980, that's just in the U.S. Isolation and condemnation of epileptics still occurs throughout the world today." Sara looked like she'd been slapped hard but these were facts she had to face.

"The demon that supposedly possessed the boy is not some spirit, it is fear. The child had grand mal seizures, that scared those who were not aware of what is happening. They are the ones possessed by fright that they transposed to the boy. The disciples were terrified and could not help him, because the fear in their faces buried him with rejection. Jesus talked about moving a mountain, he isn't talking about an earthly mountain, he is talking about the mountains we create in our minds. They are not real. When we finally have the courage to face them they vanish. Facing fear is the only way to move the mountains. Jesus can do this because he is not afraid, he knows the demon or evil spirit does not exist. The person who called you this afternoon is the one possessed, by making scripture fit for themselves, and losing track of loving others, especially the disabled. We should feel sorry for those who condemn people with epilepsy, something that is not always easy to do."

I paused for a moment, then said, "I wonder what the boy's life was like after he was cured of epilepsy. I'm sure there were those who were still scared of him and stayed away, then there were those who practiced being good Christians." I looked straight at Sara and said, "If you think about the visions many people in the Bible had, they follow the characteristics of a complex partial or absence seizures. You should turn your experience into a sermon, be honest with the congregation. Some will be lost but many will be saved."

Being a strong Christian, she smiled and thanked me for helping instill hope in her situation. I put her Bible away and gave her a kiss on the forehead as she sat, looking down at Samuel who was looking back at her and wagging his tail. I whispered in her ear, "Remember, you are the mustard seed. Most importantly, keep your faith."

She was deep in thought, so I quietly left the house and walked back to my home for the night, relieved that Trish was there with her. I was now aware that the stigma of epilepsy had been deeply implanted in Sara, a stigma that even if overcome, never goes away.

Chapter 18

Since the complex partial seizure, travel for Sara was becoming more of an issue as she feared having another seizure and losing control while driving. Trish made sure Sara's stroke neurologist was aware of her seizure and her appointment was moved up a month to the end of the week. Sara wanted me to go with her this time to explain what happened. Her arm was jerking more frequently since the seizure on Sunday making her terrified of having another that would leave her immobile, especially if it happened on the way to VCU, an area she was not familiar with. I agreed but insisted on driving. My willingness to help must have brought Sara a huge sense of peace, and this became evident as her arm stopped jerking soon after our discussion.

I was aware the doctor's understanding of what the seizure entailed was important, since there are many different treatments, and an appropriate diagnosis must be made in the few minutes allotted for the appointment. Sara told me that Dr. Anderson was her stroke neurologist, then joked about my being the neighborhood seizure expert.

The journey to VCU took several hours, but the biggest challenge and longest part of the trip was driving through the city to get to the hospital. That part alone could have triggered a seizure in anyone, but probably caused more heart attacks before that would happen. The facility itself was huge and finding a place to park took time too. We then had to walk for quite a while through a maze of hallways and staircases to get to the epilepsy center. Fortunately, we arrived right on time.

Once Dr. Anderson learned of my experience, she went into more depth about Sara's condition than she had during her last visit. We learned how remarkable Sara's recovery had been, especially her returning to work in such a complex position as running a church in a relatively short period of time. Dr. Anderson had many questions for Sara about the symptoms, especially with the feeling or lack thereof in her left arm. She then wanted to know more about the seizures, especially the complex partial. It was good I came along because Sara could explain what she felt, but not what happened.

I then said, "She loses control of her left hand and sometimes her entire arm for nearly a day or so. Most of the time, this clears up, and she is fine. This time, it spread into her leg and her eyes started roving or moving independently. She lost control of her cognitive abilities except she can still hear my voice when this occurs."

Sara listened, but she looked confused. When I finished, she asked the doctor for more information about what a seizure entailed. Dr. Anderson answered, "There are three stages to a seizure. What happens first is known as the preictal stage. This often involves an odd feeling, occasional jerking movement, memory replay, physical feeling, or an odd smell or taste. For you, this is the momentary loss of control of your left hand or arm, seeing the same thing over and over, or seeing multiple items when there is only one object you're looking at. The ictal stage is when the seizure climaxes and the person loses control of a body part or consciousness. For you, this is when what started in your left-hand spreads into your arm, leg, and face. The postictal stage involves the mind resetting itself back to normal, which often involves issues with memory recall, difficulty moving her arm or leg, and exhaustion."[*] The doctor then looked at me and said, "You seem to understand something about seizures. Did you time the ictal stage?"

I replied, "Yes, that stage lasted about three minutes. That is why I wanted to be here today, to make sure you understood everything that is happening. Through my studies and experience, I

---

[*] See appendix D for more information.

104

know to call 911 when the person having a seizure stops breathing or the seizure lasts longer than five minutes than usual. This is correct for Sara's case, is it not?"

The neurologist nodded in agreement, then added, "Sara's seizures may last for hours, so don't be surprised. They should be local, affecting her arm or leg only, but they may spread to other parts of the body, like her face. There is nothing wrong with any of these parts of the body. They are affected because the area of the brain that controls them was damaged by the stroke. When it gets excited there is an uncontrolled impulse that causes those parts of the body to contract or jerk. If she has difficulty breathing or relapses from one seizure to another, call 911."

Sara then asked about the headaches she had been having for most of her life and if there was any relationship to the stroke. Dr. Anderson got excited when she heard about this and it seemed Sara didn't realize the importance of the doctor knowing about her migraines. Dr. Anderson then asked about the triggers to the headaches then went on to explain, "Your headaches were caused by a malformation of the artery that runs from your heart to your brain, causing it to spasm and restrict the blood flow. This causes memory issues, with the headache triggered by a sudden rush of blood when the artery reopened. Seems the extraordinary stress associated with being the pastor of a church increased your blood pressure, the perfect setting for the hemorrhagic stroke. This usually cannot be detected because everything appears normal, except for that instant when it happened. The years of having migraines indicates that the stroke was bound to happen. In your case, the artery constricted, then ruptured, causing the severe bleeding between the skull and brain. This can often cause significant brain damage and much of the time, death.

"Sara, you are a miracle because the probability of survival for this type of stroke is very low. The immediate reaction of your secretary in calling 911 as she drove to the church provided the time the emergency response team and the doctors needed to save your life. Just a few minutes in this situation can mean the difference between life and death." As I listened, I wondered, *what was the role of me and Sara coming together?*

Sara's neurologist talked of several other cases which indicated she had many years of experience working with people who suffered from similar strokes. My lack of knowledge about strokes, led me to ask several questions concerning lack of blood flow to the brain, as happened to a relative of mine. This must have been a clear indication of my desire to learn, so she helped me by explaining, "There are two different types of strokes, the most common is known as an ischemic stroke and involves the blood being cut off, usually by a blood clot, this seems to be the type you are implying. Sara's was different, she had a hemorrhagic stroke which involved a sudden massive internal bleeding and resulted in swelling of the brain and increased pressure in the skull. The swelling and pressure damages brain cells and tissues. Many people die from these and the twenty-five percent who survive will develop seizures within a year. Sara's high blood pressure, high emotional and mental stress levels, and a malformation of the blood vessels coming into the brain were the most probable causes of her stroke."

She continued, "Sara is an amazing case, not only with her surviving, but also with her being able to recover so quickly." She then assured us Sara's brain was doing fine and that she was adding another medication that should prevent any more strokes or bleeding and should stop the seizures. I recognized the medication immediately because it had been given to me before to treat my seizures. The side effects were horrendous and caused me to lose my temper over the smallest things. My neurologist took me off of it immediately to protect my family. However, I kept silent because this side-effect did not happen to everyone. The doctor then looked at Sara and told her, "Because of the extent of your seizures, I want you to see one of our epileptologists. This is a doctor who specializes in treating people like you who have epilepsy." Although Sara knew she was having seizures, she seemed shocked when Dr. Anderson said, "you have epilepsy."

When Sara looked at me for my opinion, she saw my head nodding, then agreed with the doctor whose assistant proceeded with scheduling an appointment for Sara. It would be nearly another month before the epileptologist could see Sara due to that department's busy schedule.

Sara then asked about driving and the state restrictions for people diagnosed with epilepsy. Dr. Anderson explained that "this state is one of the most lenient for allowing people with seizure disorders to have a driver's license. As long as the person has a preictal warning that enables them to pull over safely or the seizures are totally under control with medication, the state allows them to drive." Sara was relieved to know that the twitching in her arm, which lasts for several hours, could serve as her warning system.

Sara was beaming as we left the office. The doctor not only instilled hope in her, she also provided assurance that the worst was over, and that Sara could still live a full life. She just needed a little more time to recover and she would be able to perform all the roles required of a pastor. It almost seemed as though she was walking on water, so filled with joy was she, as she talked of her ability to fulfill what she felt was her calling.

Over the next ten days, Sara had the same side effects to her new medication as I had. The medication changed her personality; she no longer had any patience and got upset over the smallest things. Although her left hand no longer twitched, she was dropping objects more often and seemed to have less control of her leg, impacting her ability to walk as she would occasionally trip. She fell several times and had the bruises to prove it. She was no longer the person I first met and enjoyed being with. We talked about some of the problems I had with medications changing my personality, and she was able to recognize these side effects and called Dr. Anderson to report what was happening. The doctor prescribed another medication, and she was weaned off the one she had been taking. This helped her return to her more normal disposition and to the person I could work with. Unfortunately, it was not as effective in controlling her seizures as her arm would jerk once or twice a week.

Chapter 19

It had been nearly four months since I met Sara. Her seizures now seemed under control with the medications and she was the fun-loving person I knew again, with a caring nature that was so attractive about her. However, she was finding it more and more difficult to write a sermon. What used to take one day now required two. Fridays and Saturdays became devoted to writing and preparing for the Sunday services. I knew there would be setbacks with recovery, but with time, she was having more difficulty organizing her thoughts. The ideas would come, but she just couldn't write them down. This was exacerbated by her having little to no touch in her left hand, which inhibited her ability to type. She could no longer type twenty to thirty words per minute as she once could. As she had short-term memory loss and slowness of typing or writing, she would lose a concept that would come to her mind and it would often never return, to which she became frustrated. It reminded me of when I took notes in graduate school where I wanted to jot down a concept the professor spoke about, but my short-term memory could not retain it long enough for me to write it down. Fortunately, I was assisted by other students; in Sara's case, she was on her own as the pastor.

We had been through another set of Sunday services, and I noticed, once again, her left arm twitching during the second service. She slipped out the back of the sanctuary at the end instead of going to the doorway to say goodbye to everyone individually as she typically did. I hurried back to her office and found her nearly in tears with her left arm twitching more noticeably.

While entering, I asked, "Is everything okay? Your sermon went very well."

When she heard my voice, she turned around and expressed her frustration as she sternly said, "No, I can't even get my vestment off. Can you please help me?"

This time, there was no issue with the zipper as I quickly undid the clip and pulled the zipper down. She seemed relieved and relaxed until moments later when her arm jerked again. She tensed up once more. We decided to head for home right away. We hoped this did not become a seizure like it had the last week. Instead of hoping, I should have been praying.

She was very quiet as we drove home. I wondered if I should stay with her or if it would be safe to leave her at home alone, knowing I was right next door. She seemed calmer as she returned to her living room and sat in her reclining chair. Her arm was not jerking, and she had her cell phone on her lap, just in case.

"Just let me know if you need anything. I will be painting a bedroom in my house and am less than a stone's throw away. You did terrific today. Let me pay you back, I'll plan on making dinner tonight. Get some rest now, and let your brain settle down," I said. This made her smile, she even chuckled a little, then closed her eyes as she was enveloped by exhaustion.

I gave her a kiss on the forehead and heard her quietly say "Thank you." While heading out the door, my hopes were that her seizure would settle down with the stress of the church service being in the past.

About fifteen minutes later, my cell phone chirped, notifying me of a new message. It was from Sara, and it said, "I'M HAVING A SEIZURE!" I quickly wrapped my paint brush in a rag to preserve it and ran over to her house. She wasn't in her chair, so I looked down the hallway and saw her near her bedroom where she was lying on the floor. Her left arm was twitching back and forth, she was in the advanced level of the preictal stage—the warning that a major seizure was coming. Sara was able to use her right hand and could see and hear me. For a moment, I felt nauseous as a surge of anxiety hit me, exacerbated by a momentary flashback of my own seizures, laying on the floor, able to see, but not move.

While battling for control of my own fears and emotions, I knelt and held her right hand, and managed to say in a calm voice, "I am with you, Sara. You are going to be okay. Let's get you into your bed."

Before we could even start to move, her whole left side seized as her arm and leg shook in a fast, rhythmic motion. The left side of her face became distorted as the muscles tightened, while the right side was locked with a terrifying expression. I grabbed a pillow off the bed and got it under her head as it began to bounce against the floor. I pulled my cell phone out of my pocket and activated the stopwatch to time the seizure, then started the video camera to record what was happening. I knew this typically lasted only a few minutes for most people. Fortunately, it did not affect her breathing, although she was bright red from the stress of her tightened muscles. For nearly five minutes, I watched the seizure contort the left side of her body, yet her breathing continued, and there was no indication that she may die. Throughout this period, I repeatedly assured her, "I'm with you. You are safe." Inside part of my brain, I was praying for the seizure to stop; another part I was grappling with fear. As my stopwatch was approaching the five-minute point, I turned off the camera and activated the phone, getting ready to call 911, even though the doctor had told me the seizures could last longer. My fears were intensifying as she didn't seem to be coming out of it. That was when her leg and arm stopped convulsing, and her face relaxed. I then breathed a long sigh of relief.

During her recovery, I kept telling her she was safe and stroked the hair off her face, then held her right hand. She smiled a little and slipped off into sleep. Her body was exhausted. The blanket I took off the bed helped make her more comfortable on the floor. My kneeling beside her and holding her hand seemed to bring her a sense of peace. Then suddenly she squeezed it very hard, sparking another shot of distress through me while thinking she was slipping back into another seizure. Then she said in a shallow voice, "Thank you." I managed to help her get into bed, and she slept for several more hours. It took several attempts to get a hold of Trish. She was not readily available but changed her priorities when she heard what happened and came right over, ready to spend the night with Sara.

Trish and I talked about what happened, and she said, "I noticed Sara disappeared right after the service and that her car was gone when I came out to the parking lot. I knew something was wrong but was tied up with some meetings at church that Sara was to attend. I got myself ready to come over and spend the night right after getting home. I was to help with the youth group at the church this afternoon, but we learned to have backups and someone else was able to fill in for me. Just tell me what needs to be done if Pastor Sara has another seizure."

I smiled a little and told her, "Call me, and I'll come over. Every seizure is different."

I noticed Trish's car in the driveway the following day, but since she had not contacted me, thought it best to give myself a chance to recover. It was Wednesday evening when Sara called to talk about what happened. She invited me over and we sat at her kitchen table, and I noticed her smile was back and she looked fully recovered. She started with "When I heard your voice, it brought me a sense of peace knowing you would make sure I was going to recover." She then told me what she could remember.

"You know about the problems I had during the service and your helping me get home. After you left my house that day, I thought more about what happened at the church and felt guilty about leaving without visiting with the congregation, then remembered about the meetings I was to attend. Immediately, my head began to hurt, and my arm began to jerk again. So, I sent you the text and headed for my room. I have little memory of what happened next, except hearing you come in the house and run down the hallway. Your calm voice gave me hope."

Then I shared, "As I watched you, I felt a presence telling me I was in the right place doing the right thing." Now the good feeling of providing hope came over me, knowing that she felt the presence of safety despite the storm ravaging through her brain.

I did not want to admit to her that I was scared, as she had such an intense seizure. She had reached a point where the seizures were more intense, making me think that a part of her brain died every time, or that was I reliving the battle within myself when my brain was wracked by seizures. I should have stopped wondering and lived in the present, as worrying about the future was intensifying my stress levels.

I told her how the worst case of the ictal stage for me involved my whole face becoming distorted and my entire body going rigid, and I lost all my senses except for my vision which sometimes flashed on and off throughout the seizure. This kept a part of my consciousness aware of the storm surging within me. My seizures would last ten to fifteen minutes in most cases. Through medication, my seizures were reduced to the simple partial type that involved a loss of consciousness with odd chewing and swallowing. Often, I would clap or pound my hands on a table. Sometimes the seizure affected my breathing to some extent and caused my body to turn blue, and I needed oxygen to help my recovery.

She had many questions about what happened after the seizure and what the body goes through in recovery. She was curious and scared as I told her how this involved sleep and a severe headache for both of us, except in my case my cognitive skills took a few hours to return and my long-term memory required several days to recover. I added, "This is known as the postictal stage, so you'll learn more about this when we talk to the epileptologist."

She said, "I really don't have to remember because you'll do all that for me, won't you? You're such a good soldier helping me through this. I would be lost without you."

"I'll be there, Sara. Don't worry about that. I am so happy you are back again."

I never told her that as I watched her recover, I was subconsciously recovering myself. This was triggered by my past and intensified by the pain I was feeling for her. I kept hoping there was a medication or combination of medications that would help control her seizures and let her live a full life. I really wanted her to implement her plan with the church that would enable us to work together to serve many people.

She gave me a tired smile and said, "And I am so happy to be able to give you a hug and a kiss." She wrapped her arms around me and gave me a huge hug, then said, "Good night."

I was relieved to see Trish come out of what would eventually become her room, and we smiled at each other. She was the eyes and ears of the situation and through prayer, helped to instill hope in us. Even Samuel wagged his tail at me as I headed for the kitchen door.

Chapter 20

For the next couple of weeks, we had been seeing each other nearly every day, enjoying each other's company and assistance with preparing decent meals—something difficult when living alone, yet important in preventing seizures. We even joked about building a corridor between our homes. It was early one weekday morning, when Trish had come over for a walk with Sara and to talk about some church matters. My cell phone went off soon after entering the grocery store a few miles away from home. At first, I thought that Sara was calling to add another item to the list. After swiping the answer icon, I heard her scream, "I'm having a seizure!" After swallowing hard to control my distress, I said, "Just tell me where you are." But she couldn't. The phone went blank.

I dropped my shopping basket on the floor and flew out of the building, running to my car as fast as possible. In my rush to get home, I ignored the speed limit and considered the red lights and stop signs optional. While racing back to the neighborhood I wondered how serious the seizure was and where Sara and hopefully Trish would be. I drove slowly along the main street of the neighborhood, looking down the side streets as I went by. As I reached the end of the development, I saw several people clustered together near the end of the side street. They were looking down at someone laying on the ground. One of them was sitting on the street, holding the person's head.

I quickly drove over and parked near them. Sara was lying on the street with her left leg jerking back and forth and her left arm quivering near her chest. Her face was distorted as the muscles tightened on the left side. Trish was on the ground, holding Sara's head against her chest. There was blood on her shirt from where Sara's mouth had been cut from her biting down on her lip. Trish was scared, too, her face pale, and her hands trembled. It seemed like a scene from a horror movie, running in slow motion.

As I approached everyone, I introduced myself and dropped on my knees to take Sara's hand and let her know of my presence and that she was safe. My calmness reassured everyone that she was going to be okay. We had to let the seizure pass, however. To help everyone, I felt it important to explain what was happening. Sara could hear me too. The color in Trish's face returned as she better understood my role in caring for Sara.

It had been nearly ten minutes since Sara's initial phone call to the time I arrived. The owner of a nearby home was watching and offered to help by calling an ambulance. I let him know this was not necessary based on what the neurologist had told us and her breathing to be normal. Someone asked if he had a blanket and some bottles of water for Sara and some of the other people. He acted quickly and returned with a pillow, blanket and several bottles of water, but none of which was needed or could be used at the time. Within a few minutes her seizure began to subside, her face began to regain shape, and everyone breathed a sigh of relief.

She could sit up but could not move her left arm or leg. I brought my car over right beside her, and four of us helped her into the front seat. As we were driving back to her house, I was wondering how we would get her out of the car, up the steps to her front door, and inside her home. Sara was taller than me, which made matters difficult. Trish rode in the backseat, with her hands on Sara's shoulders, assuring her she was loved and safe, and it made Sara smile. It was a very short ride and upon getting to Sara's house, the two of us tried to get her out of the car. Her left leg was useless, and we needed to lift her out, but could not. She could not even lift her left arm up to help us. We felt hopeless for a moment.

Suddenly, four other people were there to help us, two of whom were very big men who lifted Sara out of the car and made sure she was safely in the house. I was behind her as they brought her in the through the front door and I guided them to a couch where she could lie down. I knelt beside her, and she smiled again. She apologized for not offering anything to us as she said, "Sorry. I have a headache."

Everyone laughed. It was great to have her back again. It would take several more hours before she could walk and use her left arm. She was exhausted and slept the rest of the day, waking occasionally to ask for a drink and talked of having a headache, which was expected.

When I got up and turned around, the people who had helped us were suddenly gone. My first impression was they were angels who appeared when we were in need. When going outside to close the doors on my car, however, I recognized some of the men as they were across the street working on a house and went over to thank them. The youngest, who was in his early twenties, saw me approaching and laid down his tools. He walked over to me to ask me how the "lady" was doing. As the others came up to me, I thanked them all and let them know Sara was going to be fine. The young fellow told me about his experience caring for his mother who had epilepsy, and when he saw us struggling to get Sara out of the car, had yelled to the rest of the crew to follow him. They then ran across the street, and arrived just in time to help. He did not know she had had a seizure, but he had an intuition that we were in trouble. I still considered them as angels who arrived to help in the midst of our ordeal.

After walking back to the house my thoughts were on Trish, for she looked like she had been in a fight. She was pale, looked tired, and had Sara's blood on her blouse. She needed to go home to get cleaned up and rest, so I offered to stay with Sara. When Trish returned, she smiled and hugged me as her thanks for appearing in the middle of her crisis. We then talked about what happened and I wanted to see if she could continue to help. "It was amazing you were able to respond the way you did," I told her.

Her smile disappeared as she replied, "Watching her have a seizure with blood dripping out of her mouth was terrifying because I was imagining her dying while holding her. I couldn't even think to call you back and let you know where we were, I'm so sorry." She looked away and went quiet for a moment. I could see she was thinking about what happened. It was best for me to keep quiet and give her time to process the trauma she experienced. She then continued, "Your calmness and knowledge of what to do brought me out of the panic I was in. I don't know what I would have done if you had not come along. Now I know about epilepsy and what to do, but I'm still scared, and question my ability to react appropriately."

I responded, "God put you in the right place at the moment someone was in need. You are a brave and blessed woman, and I thank you for your willingness and courage to help. You need to get away for a while and let your mind get occupied with something less dramatic. Is there someone who could fill in for a couple of days?"

"I know someone who can help. I'll stay until they come. Thank you, and God bless you." After a short pause she said, "I need a hug." That seemed easy to do and was a tremendous help to me as well, and it helped the smiles return to our faces.

As soon as everyone was safe and Trish's replacement understood what to do, I walked home. On the way, I thought about a time when I had a seizure and felt hopeless and alone. I hoped Sara realized there were people here to help her through all this.

When I saw her the next day, she was doing much better, and we talked about notifying her doctors of the seizure. I let her know I could take her to any appointments she might have. Later that day, we went for a walk to thank the people who had rendered assistance. We rang the doorbell of the man who had provided the blanket and water. He came out to talk with us about his experience and appreciation that I knew what to do. His wife had died a few weeks earlier after she had collapsed near where Sara had her seizure, and he was reliving what had happened when he saw Sara collapse. He feared Sara was dying and he thought of his wife while rushing out the door to help.

As we told him some of our story about our ministries, brain injury, epilepsy, and strokes, then meeting each other as neighbors, he looked at us with a smile. He told us how God had brought him and his wife together and was now witnessing God working with the two of us. He thanked us for sharing our stories as it brought him even closer to God, and he reminded us to cherish the moment.

We came across several other people who had seen what had happened the day before. Some came over to check on how Sara was doing, many of whom told us of how they prayed for her while they witnessed what happened. A few turned their backs and walked away, however. The one I remembered the most was the woman who was watering her flowers but when she recognized us, she dropped her hose and ran into her house.

Chapter 21

Summer was nearly over, and we were looking forward to the Fall weather and the cooler temperatures. It had been four weeks since we had seen Sara's stroke doctor. During that time, she had two complex partial seizures and several simple seizures that affected her arm and vision. I was concerned because they were lasting longer each time. The appointment with the epileptologist seemed to take forever to come. As the appointment approached, we talked about what the doctor would expect, and Sara was relieved I would provide her with transportation. She also was appreciative of my willingness to be there to answer the doctor and to ask the appropriate questions.

On the day of the appointment, she came over to my house early in the morning so we could make the long drive to the VCU Epilepsy Center and get lunch along the way. She was nervous and afraid of the outcome and the possibility of losing her driver's license due to the most recent seizures. She was prepared to argue that she had a warning system in the jerking of her arm that would allow her to pull over and seek help if needed.

Dr. Leyde, the epileptologist, was kind, yet to the point with what was happening in Sara's brain, and was very interested in how long the seizures lasted and how they progressed. We talked about what action should be taken and if I should call for emergency assistance with her seizures lasting so long. She assured both of us that since she could still breathe regularly and had not been hurt, calling 911 was not necessary.[*] As she heard this, Sara looked at me and smiled.

---

[*] There are many reasons why calling 911 during a seizure is necessary. For more information, see appendix A.

Dr. Leyde then assured Sara that her situation was treatable. Although she was taking a seizure medication prescribed by the stroke specialist, it was obvious this was not enough. Sara was then prescribed another medication and was told the importance of taking it appropriately and consistently. She would also coordinate the treatment with Dr. Anderson, the stroke specialist. She listened to Sara express the problems she was having with writing sermons and assured her that her memory would improve once the seizures were under control. It seemed like everything would go well with little effort and gave us hope as she talked of her experience treating patients having similar types of seizures after a stroke.

I thought this would make Sara feel better, but then I saw her sit up straight and look directly at the doctor as she asked, "What about my driving?"

The doctor's response gave her peace of mind. "Well, the jerking of your arm provides a warning system that your seizures are coming. Since this happens hours before your seizures break through, you should have the ability to know when not to drive. You are to limit your driving to local trips where help is nearby. However, if your arm starts to jerk or has done so at any time of the day, you are not to drive! Now, since you seem to have this jerking motion nearly every day and we're starting another medication, you are not to drive for 30 days, as it takes a while to for the dosage to build up in your body."

Sara's visible sense of relief was replaced with an expression of frustration when the doctor mentioned the initial suspension. I felt the frustration myself when thinking about Sara's need for me and Trish to help her, especially with work. She seemed to force a smile as she thanked the doctor for her help and consideration.

For treatment, Dr. Leyde recommended Sara go through the five-day EEG monitoring at the hospital. Sara knew through my experience that this is where a person lives within the boundaries of a hospital room, with a bunch of wires attached to their head that are tied into a computer system through a conduit in the ceiling. The only privacy was in the bathroom, and even that was limited so the nurses can hear and respond if Sara were to have a seizure. Baths and showers would not be allowed throughout the test. The only difference between her test and mine was that someone, be it friend or family, had to be in the room with her.

As we drove home, Sara seemed very relieved. She could not believe how she was now able to obtain the treatment necessary for her to gain control of her seizures and she could function as a pastor again. She was filled with hope and continued to be amazed about my interest in helping her and my dedication to getting her the right treatment. She then asked if I could be the person to stay with her during the EEG. Initially, it thought it was a good idea and, without thinking, assured her of my availability.

Then I remembered the flashbacks I had when I first took Sara to the hospital—when she came to see me with her eyes moving independently of each other, and seeing Samuel repeatedly run down the hallway—and this indicated to me my accompanying her would not be a good idea. A few days after we returned from the epileptologist appointment, flashbacks of my experience during my week-long EEG began to occur, confirming that there was no way I could stay with Sara for five days. It would make me feel like I was going back to where my surgery took place, wracked by seizures which occurred several times a day. This time, the feeling of defeat came as I watched her suffer seizures over and over again. For both of us, it was better that I did not accompany her.

It was a month before the extended EEG was to take place. Sara contacted Emily, her niece, who agreed to be the one to stay with her the whole time. I felt a sense of relief and agreed to take care of Samuel while she was at the hospital.

Chapter 22

I remembered the hopes I once shared with Sara. A rush of anxiety hit me as I returned to the present, and my fears returned. I knew the audience needed to understand what happened when we went sailing together for the first time, so I had to explain it well.

Sara still managed to do well with her sermons by utilizing her resources and her staff. My ignorance of what she was supposed to do and what I witnessed at the services made me think she had control of her work. I was not aware of how her organizational disability had increased, impacting her ability to do everything that was expected by the church. To escape the reality of it all, we had been talking about our desire to go sailing. Fall had arrived and it was a good time in the year to buy a boat.

I had many years of experience with all types of sailboats. In fact, I had crewed on some of the fastest small sailboats, the kind that were less than eighteen feet long with no protection from the elements. They required a lot of physical effort to keep them upright because the weight of the crew was the counterbalance to the force of the wind that wanted to flip them over. Those small boats became more difficult to sail because physical exhaustion set in earlier and my reaction time was slowing down with age. There were days my friend and I spent more time in the water trying to upright a boat than sailing it. It was time to step up to the more stable—cruising or liveaboard class.

I needed a crew who could go on a cruise on for several days (or months) and enjoy the sailing and environment more than the thrill. Sailing had been the lifesaver of my mental health, as I enjoyed being on the water, powered by the wind, a force that can't be seen. It made me feel closer to God and to heaven. Sara became excited as she told me, "I will have to be the skipper since you have no experience sailing such a high-class boat." As her face lit up, she said, "I will definitely have to teach you how to sail the one you get."

I jokingly replied, "Yes, sir. I mean, *ma'am*!"

After shopping for several months, I found the perfect boat the week before Thanksgiving. It was twenty-eight feet long and set up for one person to operate. We were overjoyed the day I got it. It had a twenty-horsepower diesel engine with a cruising range of greater than 180 miles when under power. The sails were rigged, so the jib was wrapped around the forestay, making the size easily adjustable, depending on how strong the wind was blowing. The main took some effort to raise and lower; however, it was rigged with a self-gathering system when being lowered, so a single person could do it. A person could sail it by themselves, but two or three would be much easier.

The galley had a refrigerator and freezer, alcohol stove, and plenty of cabinet space. A gas grill hung off one side of the transom for cooking with little cleanup required. There was plenty of sleeping space for several people, and all the ports or windows could be opened and had screens. It was designed to be a complete home if I wanted to live on the water.

The best and most important component was the self-navigation system. While using engine or sail, a computer could be activated, which took over the steering and kept the boat on course. The importance of this feature would become evident in a few months. The owner had become disabled and could no longer use the boat; it was his love, and selling it was very difficult for him. He felt relieved knowing I would take good care of it and it would be used often. Eventually, it became my mental health recovery vehicle.

Sara was watching the weather, and early one morning, she came running over to report, "It's supposed to be in the low sixties this afternoon, getting colder this evening. Let's go for a short sail!"

I gave her that skeptical look and she assured me, "I'm doing fine and have taken my medication." I then grinned and responded, "Aye, aye, captain."

We both grabbed our windbreaker jackets and headed for the boat. The boat had not been outfitted with any food, tools, warm clothing, blankets, or jackets—some of the basic needs if something were to happen while underway.

The wind was blowing down the river, and we knew from the chart that the channel was narrow for half a mile past the bridge that crossed the river, near the marina where the boat was kept. The temperature was warm, and it felt fantastic to be out on the water. We managed to get the boat out of the slip, and it performed well as we maneuvered out of the port and sailed down the river. Sara looked like she was in heaven, and her face was beaming as she stood behind the wheel. She had total control of the boat.

As the day wore on, she taught me many aspects of sailing with an emphasis on the names of all the parts of the boat and sections of the sails. She knew this was difficult for me due to my lobectomy when part of the memory control center was removed. She had to repeat the names of the components several times before it would stick in my mind. I was so grateful of her understanding and patience that I forgot to keep track of the time and how far we had travelled.

The position of the sun was off to the west quite a ways as I told her, "We need to head back to the dock. As the sun sets, it will get very cold again, and the forecast tonight is for temperatures in the upper twenties."

Knowing that we would be going nearly straight upwind as we returned, she recommended we drop the sails and motor back. Everything was going well until the engine lost cooling water and overheated. The overheat alarm went off, and I knew we were in trouble. My stomach tightened with worry. We were now without an engine.

I quickly ran forward and dropped anchor to keep us from drifting onto a shoal. I called the towing service only to learn they did not operate in our area. To make matters worse, we were the only boat out on the water at that time of year. We discussed our situation and agreed to try to sail back. It was going to be a lot of work as we had to go upwind and would have to tack many times.[*] I went up to the mast and raised the mainsail. Sara took the helm as I went forward and raised the anchor. Neither of us said a word as we both understood how serious our situation was. I never told her that I was downright scared because I didn't have any experience on how the boat handled going upwind and how to change course. Sara became quiet and very serious. The wind picked up to twenty miles an hour, and it suddenly felt colder.

With our first tack, we wound up going too far downwind as I oversteered, not knowing how the boat would respond to the helm. We lost almost all our progress. We were learning more and more with each tack, especially how difficult it was to steer twelve thousand pounds and twenty-eight feet of boat. It seemed to take forever to respond to our turning the wheel. The wind continued to strengthen, and it got much colder as the sun was setting.

We were actually doing better with each tack and were close to the bridge where the channel shifted and became very narrow. We looked at each other and Sara seemed exhausted and scared. I wondered what I looked like as the tension increased inside of me. She was working too hard and was due her medication. Much longer and she could slip into a seizure.

---

[*] To go upwind in a sailboat requires sailing as close to the direction of the wind as possible, then turn into the wind and head as close as possible going the other direction. The sailor's terminology for this maneuver is to *tack*; going back and forth as the boat goes upwind is known as *tacking*.

I looked at her and said, "It is going to get very difficult from now on in this narrow channel. We will have to do even better than before."

I could see exhaustion in her face, cognizant that it was a key trigger to her seizures, and I began to fear the worst. The channel was less than a hundred feet wide now, and we had to tack every three to four minutes. Sara did her best but could not keep it up as she had no energy left and could no longer crank in the jib. I soon oversteered, and we ran aground in the shallow water just outside the channel. We were now stuck, less than one hundred yards from the bridge, and the winds were continuing to increase, now blowing over twenty-five miles an hour. Not only were we exhausted, we were cold. Sara went below as I dropped the anchor and the sails to keep us from drifting farther onto the shoal.

It was nearly dark. We had no food, blankets, extra jackets, and most importantly, medication. If we did not get help and had to stay the night, we would be very cold, and Sara would certainly be having seizures. My cell phone worked, so I called Jennifer to tell her about our situation. All I remember her saying was "Oh my god! What should we do?" She then said, "Let me call the Coast Guard and the police. They can come and get Sara off the boat." She called me back a few minutes later to tell me, "They will not respond unless there is a life in danger. I told them about Sara's condition, and they said they would only come if she was having a seizure."

"Dear god! It will take them more than an hour to get here, and if she slips into a seizure, she could be dead by then," I replied. Little did I know that Sara heard me.

I then called the previous owner to tell him of our situation and to see if he knew how to get help. He apologized and said he felt responsible. He started calling friends and found some men who would come in a powerboat and tow us into the dock. The temperature inside the boat was now less than thirty-five degrees. Outside, the wind chill brought it down into the twenties. I looked at Sara as she sat on the forward berth, shaking from the cold. My adrenaline was pumping as I worried about her seizures, unknowingly keeping me warm.

Eventually, I saw some lights on the water, and signaled with the light on my cell phone. The tide had come in, and the boat had broken free from the mud. It was now held at station by the anchor. As the other boat approached, I went on deck and handed them a line to tow us in. The wind and tide made it difficult to point us in the right direction, and everyone feared both boats would run aground on another shoal as we were blown across the channel. Fortunately, the tide was exceptionally high as the strong winds pushed more water up the river and made it deep enough for the boats to clear and pass over the shoal. We finally made it back to the channel, and within fifteen minutes, we were safe in the harbor and tied to a dock.

I thanked the men for rescuing us and offered to pay them for their efforts. The captain of the boat responded, "No, sir, we will not take your money. We could have been in the same situation. As boaters, we depend on one another. Glad we could be of help."

All I could say was "Thank you," over and over. I was shivering very hard from the cold and needed to get moving again.

As I took care of closing up the boat, Sara went to the car to get warm. My arms and legs were completely worn out. I was in tears from the exhaustion caused by the work, stress, and low temperatures, but most of all by my worry about Sara having a seizure at any minute. It had been nearly three hours since her medication needed to have been taken, and her body temperature must have been decreasing. She said she was cold but that she was okay when she got into the car and started the engine. She remembered she had a dose of her medication in the glove compartment and took it. I breathed a sigh of relief and returned to the boat to make sure everything was secure.

We then drove to Jennifer's, where she had a hot dinner waiting for us. She was greatly relieved when I called her to say we were back at the dock. She wanted to hear more about what happened, and we both looked at her and said we were too tired to talk about it. In actuality, I did not want Sara reliving what had happened. At that moment, I felt a rush of anxiety overcome me and nausea rose in my stomach. This used to happen just prior to me having a grand mal seizure. Fortunately, it passed without disabling me, but my hands were shaking, and my speech was slightly impaired. I gave an excuse that the trembling was due to muscle exhaustion, which was not totally false.

Soon after dinner, we drove home. Sara looked much better and said she was fine as she entered her house. Now I could relax some as I no longer was fully responsible for her care. As my stress level decreased, exhaustion took over and I fell into a deep sleep on my bed, too tired to change my clothes.

Early the next morning, Jennifer called me. "I need to check on you now that I am out of my panic mode. You looked so stressed out last night. I swear, there were new strain lines carved into your face. I just knew you were going to have a seizure yourself."

I didn't tell her that I came close to actually having one. Instead, I laughed and responded, "Yeah, and you looked like you just read your little brother's obituary."

Now that everyone was safe, she laughed too. "I didn't realize you were that scared of losing your boat."

As I heard this, I felt distressed, and I went quiet for a while. She thought I was upset and hung up on her. To check if I was still on the line, she asked, "Are you okay? I lost you."

"Sorry for going quiet. What I really feared was losing Sara, especially as she was without her medication and stuck on the boat. I just pictured a seizure coming, and there was nothing I could do but wait and hope. My god, what would I have done watching her have a seizure and not being able to respond or get help." I went silent again. Jennifer knew I had more to say and quietly waited for me to continue. "Sorry I dumped on you, sister. I know the boat could be replaced, but what about Sara?"

"Little brother, I sense you are falling in love with her. Be careful. Just as you tell your clients who are struggling to be caregivers, you have to take care of yourself!"

"Thanks, sister. Now you are telling me to practice what I preach! Being stuck on the boat made me realize my level of responsibility and the risk involved. I just can't imagine losing Sara to seizures and want to be sure she is always safe."

"Matt, just remember we are here to help each other. Call me anytime!"

As I switched off my phone, I was open to telling Sara how much I cared for her. I knew she was scared about her seizures because I was too. Even so, I wanted her to know our relationship could continue to grow. Over the next few weeks, we managed to go sailing a few times without any issues, and it was wonderful to be with her. She was a very good sailor. The engine cooling system had been repaired, and the boat outfitted with all the necessary supplies, including medications, to survive a few nights if something happened.

During our experience on that cold night, she told me how my caring created a desire for her to work hard in learning techniques that would help with her recovery. Even though she fell several times on the boat because of the loss of her sense of touch in her left hand and foot, she always smiled at me and said, "If you could recover, so can I." Sometimes her left hand just let go of what she was holding, and when I looked at her, I'd hear, "I'm learning." As we came physically close while putting the sails away at the end of each trip, she would lovingly give me a big hug and a kiss. That was when the sparkle in her eyes became brighter as she looked deep into my soul, and my heart lit up as well.

Chapter 23

Sara was now having difficulty organizing her medications and needed Tracy to do a review of her daily pill holder, which held two weeks of medications, to be sure she had everything correct. Many of the medications looked similar, and she struggled with keeping track of the containers they came in. There were a few times she had taken the same medication twice, making her sick from an overdose of one medication while missing the dose of another. Part of this problem was the stress she created for herself as she feared missing a medication, resulting in her having a seizure. This fear grows with time leading to an obsession that becomes debilitating, which is worse than a seizure itself.

I knew through experience that the more people you meet who have the same condition and issues can be the best treatment in controlling such fear. There were several people I had worked with who became great examples of this. FaceTime became a convenient tool that enabled Sara to associate closely with these individuals and learn to control her obsession caused by apprehension.

The first call was to Megan, who was excited to see us, and we had a long talk. Megan had been dealing with seizures for over sixty years and had nearly died several times. Yet she never let it stop her from her goal of being a loving mother and from sailing. Within just an hour of conversation, Sara felt like she had known Megan for many years. Megan's example and demonstrated desire to live was the model Sara needed. Megan talked of how I helped her as a mentor and how Sara should not let go of me. Sara's face lit up with a huge smile and assured Megan she would never let go as I felt her hand tighten warmly around mine.

Megan told us how difficult it could be for couples where one person was dealing with epilepsy. She told us how she and Tom were married illegally in 1974. When Tom went to get the marriage license, there was a note on the form that said anyone diagnosed with epilepsy could not be married in the state they lived in. Megan was torn, and Tom was astounded. They both agreed it would be the only time they would ever lie to obtain a license and completed the form without mention of her seizures.[*]

It seemed Megan and Sara wanted to talk about many other topics aside from epilepsy, so I left the room. They talked for several hours as Sara was excited to know how Megan was able to continue to sail big boats even as she struggled with seizures. When they were done, Sara looked very happy and relieved. I felt relieved too and told her that there was someone else for her to talk to the next day. Her name was Chris, and she was a stroke survivor.

When I saw Sara the next morning, she seemed happy even though her arm jerked occasionally. She had just taken her medications and knew it would eventually stop. She was smiling, almost beaming, as she looked at her arm and, for the first time, said, "This is nothing, and I know it will go away." This time, the medication worked, and the seizure stopped. For the first time in quite a while she was excited for the day to begin.

Later in the morning, we called Chris. She and Sara had both suffered similar hemorrhagic strokes and disabilities, except Chris did not have any seizures. I did not even need to stay around to start the discussion, as they went into it right away. Later, Sara shared how they talked of their recovery times and how Chris still had a numb place in the middle of her back. Her stroke occurred nearly ten years ago while giving birth to one of her children. No one saw it coming but as she was already in the hospital, her life was saved. I had met Chris years earlier. When I learned of her story, I could not imagine how her husband felt as he was handed their second child but watching his wife nearly die.

----

[*] The last of these laws in the United States was repealed in 1980.

Sara really appreciated learning how someone else recovered from their stroke. She wasn't smiling as much as when she had talked to Megan; however, talking with Chris made her even more hopeful of recovery. She even told me, "Now I know why you are so focused on inspiring hope in other people. You sure were successful with me." She gave me a hug for so long I wondered if she was ever going to let go. As she walked away, I heard her singing for the first time. For the next several months, it was not unusual to hear her singing some cheerful or inspiring song in her house or on the boat.

I had drifted off into the past and was smiling as I imagined hearing Sara sing again.

Chapter 24

It was the best time to fish in the late Fall as the fish were coming in to spawn. Sara no longer felt up to going fishing with me anymore, but my self-confidence had grown and my fear of going out in the boat alone faded. One morning, it was still dark as I got into my truck and started down the road to one of the tributaries where my nephew told me the drum fish run. I launched the boat, as it was a beautiful but chilly morning. The dawn came as the red, orange, and light-blue colors appeared in the eastern sky and the stars of the night were still seen in the west. There was no wind, and the waters were very calm. For the next few hours, I slowly trawled along the secret place my nephew had shown me along the edge of the river where the fish were typically found.

Hooking a bass was exciting as the fish jumped out of the water and battled being reeled in. The drum fish were different. They would fly out of the water, and I had to fight harder to bring them in. Pulling too hard made the hook come out and it took perfect timing to know when to set the hook and start the fight.

The secret place was along the shoreline and that day the fish weren't there. Another place I was going to try was in the channel and I trawled there slowly, with a lure near the bottom. I believed it would still be uneventful, but felt better with my chances, having already tried everywhere else that morning. I started to dream up some fish tales to tell Sara when I got home.

Suddenly, the rod bent way over, and my initial thought was the lure was snagged on a submerged tree limb or stump. I loosened the drag on the reel to let the line play out as I turned the boat around to go back to where the lure was snagged. Coming from the opposite direction would usually cause the lure to break free, but this time, what I assumed to be a tree trunk kept moving away. Now knowing it was a fish, I tightened the drag to make it work harder to pull the line out, careful not to tighten the twenty-pound test line past its limit. The fish kept to the bottom while swimming away and pulling the boat slowly along. Like with my seizures, it took concentration to be able to work through the battles, but I thought that this battle was one I would not be able to endure.

For the next twenty minutes, the fish kept going. I had no idea what type of fish it could be because it stayed near the bottom. As the line loosened, I'd reel in the slack, then the fish would jerk it with a sudden pull, and fifty feet of line went screeching off the reel.

It had been more than forty minutes since it had taken the lure and I could tell by the angle of the line that the fish was coming towards the surface. It was now only two to three feet underwater, and I could make out its shape. I still could not tell what type of fish it was except that there was a *very big* fish on my line. It then dove back to the bottom and overwhelmed the drag on the reel.

We were both tiring out and the tension on the line finally forced the fish to the surface. The fins broke the water fifty feet away, and the fish headed straight for the boat. I had to reel the line in fast to eliminate any slack and to prevent the hook from coming loose. The fish then shot across the bow and circled the boat. I had to run to the stern and shove the tip of the rod deep into the water to prevent the line from being cut by the propeller. The fish looped the boat twice and then went deep again, the reel shrieked as the line was pulled off. I did not know who was tired the most, the fish or me, as my arms ached from holding the rod and working the reel for nearly ninety minutes. While working on reeling the fish in once more, I thought of the battle Sara fought with her seizures. We would be close to having her seizures under control, then suddenly it was like the seizures would run away from reach, drawing everything out of her like the line screaming off my reel. I refused to give up; what I tried to determine was how much I could endure versus how long the fish could last before exhausting. The old military maxim "Never quit" came to my mind while thinking about the fish and Sara.

This time, the fish did not remain for long on the bottom and drifted to the surface. It circled slowly on the starboard side and came within inches of the boat. My arms were exhausted, and I could not get the net in place as it approached the first time. It came around again, and this time, I dropped the net right in front of it as it came by; the fish filled the large net with more than a third of it still sticking out the entry. My arms ached so much that it was impossible to lift the net, so I dropped the rod and got on my knees where I could use my back to pull it out of the water. I was able to roll the fish over the side of the boat, and dropped it on the deck, tangled in netting and line with the lure hanging out of its mouth. We both lay on the deck gasping for air and totally exhausted. It had been nearly two hours of fighting, and we both stared at each other, its red color and the black dot near the tail indicated that it was a red drum.

It would take a while to clear the fish from the netting and get the lure out of its mouth. I took some photos and texted Tim regarding the size limitations and I was extremely disappointed to learn the maximum size was twenty-eight inches. This one was forty-two inches and weighed over thirty pounds. As I lifted it from the deck, it did not move as I slowly lowered it into the water. Even when submerged, it still didn't move. That's when I said quietly, "Don't die on me now," a statement that would be used many times over during the next few months. As the water flowed through the gills of the fish, the tail began to move, and it was time to release it. I was overcome with sadness as I watched it slowly swim toward the bottom of the river.

The boat needed to be cleaned up, the rod stowed, and the net put away. I worked slowly due to my exhaustion, to the point of being tedious. Suddenly, behind me, I heard a splash and saw fins on the surface as the fish swam in a tight circle on the port side. It swam a circle three times, as if thanking me for the challenge and giving back its life; then it dove to the bottom, never to be seen again. I stood there for several minutes as I watched the ripples fade away, a part of me disbelieved what I had witnessed, while another part was enthralled by such a spiritual experience. I was jolted back to reality as I realized we had traveled several miles during the fight, and it was a long ride back to the boat ramp.

I didn't realize at that time there were similarities of the long fight with this red drum and the struggle with the seizures Sara suffered. In her case, the fight was against the electrical storm in her brain and I was there to help her regain her life as she recovered. Similar to my battle with the fish, I would reach the point of exhaustion, yet never gave up hope for Sara, always praying she would recover and be released from her seizures forever. Helping Sara taught me about the physical and mental exhaustion a caregiver must endure to help someone close to them fight the battles of epilepsy. Could the line of our love for each other hold us together, or would it be severed? This I did not know, but for this moment in time, I still thought, *Never Quit*.

Abruptly I was brought back in the present moment and found myself looking around the auditorium. There was complete silence; for a moment, I thought the room was empty. Then I heard several people sniffle as my hearing returned, and I could see the people in the seats in front as my eyes adjusted to the light which had been turned back up. I had not realized my eyes were closed as I was reliving the moment of catching the fish while telling the story.

My mouth was dry, and I signaled to Carol that I needed a drink. She came over to me with a bottle of water in her hand and told everyone we were going to take a ten-minute break. As she approached, she said, "This is an amazing story. Did it really happen?"

I replied, "Yes, it did. It was one hell of a fight."

She responded with "Oh my god!" as she looked toward the ceiling for a moment, amazed. "What an incredible experience you had!"

She handed me the water bottle, and it felt good to take a drink and remedy the dryness of my mouth. I was surprised my mouth had become so dry because until now my flowing tears kept it saturated. I took another drink, then took a deep breath and I was ready to continue. I looked at everyone in the auditorium and said, "One of the key stressors that trigger seizures is limited transportation and the distress of isolation."

Chapter 25

Sara had no extensive seizures for nearly two weeks, although she did have a few that caused her arm to jerk. The jerking of her arm was a warning for her not to drive for twenty-four hours. She agreed to follow the requirements set by the epileptologist that included the local travel restrictions and making sure she took her medications. I had to ask, "How well are you doing getting to the gym and to your meetings?"

"I am getting more concerned," she replied. "What will I do if my car breaks down or I have a seizure? I thought I was doing well until the doctor told me the jerking in my arm is my warning of a seizure. It happens once or twice a day now but hasn't spread as before and hasn't taken control of my body."

"Then maybe you should give up driving," I said hesitantly.

"I can't do that. I felt like such a burden on you and others when I couldn't drive for a month."

A week later, she was running errands, including a stop at the gym, when her arm started to twitch. She immediately pulled onto a side street and parked, then grabbed her phone and dialed her emergency contact: *me*. A feeling of dread came over me when my phone rang, and her name appeared. When I answered, I heard her scream, "I'm having a seizure!"

My initial thought was, *Oh god, not again!* And then I heard her yell the same plea once more into the phone. As much as I wanted to scream with her, I calmly asked, "Where are you?"

"I'm near Jennifer's, one block past her street, near Main Street."

I ran to my car and drove over to her. The ten minutes to get to her seemed like an eternity; her seizures seemed to last forever now.

When I arrived, she was having a partial complex seizure in the front seat, which affected the left half of her body with her limbs jerking. Only this time, her whole face was grossly distorted. As I held her right hand, her muscles started to constrict as I noticed her grip flexed on a rhythmic basis. The seizure had spread throughout her brain and was affecting her entire body. She could still hear, and her vision flickered like a damaged light bulb. I assured her, "I am here. You are safe. I will not leave you." I repeated this over and over, as I did not know if she could hear me and because I could not think of anything else to say. There seemed to be a terrible battle going on within her and I struggled within myself.

I knew she heard and understood me when the right side of her body relaxed slightly. I witnessed the rest of the seizure which lasted another fifteen minutes, wondering if her hearing my voice had helped to shorten it. Now a fear ran through me as I thought of how much longer her body could have taken before suffering extensive muscle injury. My fears triggered a high level of anxiety, and my reasoning skills were impaired as I was consumed by the most unlikely thing to happen to Sara: significant brain damage or death. My counselor training helped me keep myself together. As the anxiety subsided, I reestablished the ability to fully reason what was happening and enabled me to regain control of my emotions, especially the fear.

As the seizure subsided, Sara's eyes started to move together as she looked around, trying to establish where she was. I kissed her on her forehead, and she gave me a shallow smile as the muscles in her face relaxed. Her ability to speak clearly and comprehend anything I said was still inhibited.

"You're okay. Your brain needs some time to reset. I look forward to having you back again." I kept smiling, even though I was afraid that a stroke was impending, and recovery would not happen.

Sara could not be moved out of the driver's seat because she still had no control of her arm or leg. It took another forty minutes until she had regained the ability to move on her left side and was able to slide into the passenger seat. I then drove her to my sister's house just a few blocks away. Sara needed help getting out of the car but was able to walk up the steps with the support of the two of us. Seeing that Sara was improving, Jennifer took over, and I ran back to get my car. I ran hard to get the anxiety and frustration over her seizure out of my mind.

Gasping for air from running, I jumped in my car and pulled on my seat belt. Another flashback of my seizures hit me hard while I turned the key.

The next thing I knew, I was driving on a highway. It was dark, and there was the outline of tall trees on the side of the road. I felt anxious, and my heart began to race. The preictal nausea came, and the trees suddenly seemed closer to the road. The nausea continued to escalate, and fear took hold of me. I pulled onto the side of the road, slid the gearshift into park, and I have no memory of what happened for the next several minutes. As I recovered, there was blood dripping out of my mouth onto my shirt, and my head ached. My vision was blurry, and it took some time for me to realize that one of my contact lenses was missing. I had no idea where I was or, for that matter, why I was behind the wheel of a car. I began to win the battle for control of my mind, and slowly my other senses returned.

I then realized I had a flashback to a very dark time. I shook my head to bring myself back to the present. Even as I came back to reality, my heart was racing, and my head ached. The flashback triggered an aura, and a wave of nausea ripped through my body. Since it didn't seem to push me into unconsciousness, I drove my car to Jennifer's. When Jennifer saw me come through the front door, I noticed her mouth fell agape, and she quickly looked away. Within an hour, Sara was able to fully walk again and be back to her old self. It was nice she had recovered and was able to laugh about what had happened, even though she had a bad headache. I drove her home in her car and helped her get into the house and safely to her favorite chair.

Jennifer followed so she could drive me back to her house and I could get my car. Along the way, I told her how I felt as I watched Sara have her seizure and about my flashback afterwards. She was concerned with how this affected me as she said, "I am not sure what to say. You didn't look too good when you came into my house. You were flushed, and your face was drawn. You're not doing well, are you?"

Finally, I told her, "It drained me hard, but I have to get back to the house to be available for Sara. What if she has another seizure and no one is there to take care of her?"

Jennifer, in a raised voice, replied, "If Sara has another seizure, you call me! I will be there with you immediately! I know what you are going through because I saw you have a grand mal seizure at my home several years ago. I just saw the one seizure, and it still scares me. How many seizures have you seen Sara have now? Ten? Twenty?" She was afraid of what the stress was doing to me and knew that it was a trigger to my seizures.

It was a good question, and it forced me to think about what I had seen and endured. "I have seen Sara have some forty simple partial seizures and at least ten complex grand mals." Neither Jennifer nor I slept well that night as we relived the past in our dreams and feared the uncertainty of the future.

The next day, I had Sara call Dr. Leyde, her epileptologist to tell him about the seizure. Her medication was increased again, and there were no signs of any seizures for many days. We were starting to believe the medication was effective and talked of some sailing trips and her ability to work. When she was getting dressed, her left hand would jerk occasionally, and she would not be able to button her pants for a short while, then she would be able to again. I tried to encourage her by explaining how the nerves take a long time to heal and that this is normal and that she should expect to have full control of her hand again soon. Within a few days, the jerking completely stopped, but I still had the fear of her having another seizure and reliving my past. From then on, every time she texted or called me, I feared the worst, expecting to hear, or the message to read, "I'm having a seizure!"

Chapter 26

It was a rainy, cold Saturday morning, when we found ourselves sitting in our favorite chairs in my living room, talking about some of our other interests. Sara started it off, "We talked about sailing and seizures so much, I'd like to know a little more about you, what other travels have you been on recently?"

This did not require much thought as I replied, "I love the national parks, my favorites are in Utah. Where else can you drive for hours and see such beautiful landscapes where man is not dominated or controlled? In Utah, you can drive for hours and see no sign of humankind, outside of the roads and a few cars. You also get to see how little mankind has changed anything. I've heard some people refer to it as God's Country."

She quickly followed up with, "I have lived on both sides of the country but have not spent much time in that area. I was a very young child when my parents took us to see some of the parks out there."

"Do you have any interest in going again?" I asked.

"Maybe. What was so special about it for you?"

"For hundreds of miles, you see outcroppings of the earth along the earthquake fault lines. Huge mountains covered with snow at the top that fade into the clouds. Then there are the plateaus, thousands of feet high. The surfaces consist of fractured and broken rock that create towers or massive walls that shear straight up thousands of feet. The colors are by layer and contain pink, blue, green, black, and pure white. Most of the surface has small pine trees and brush along with cacti and some of the most beautiful flowers. Amazing how they grow out of the rock. Seeing this made me realized how insignificant we as people really are."

I could see that Sara was thinking about somewhere in Utah as she was relating to my story. I continued, "One of the parks I went to was Canyonlands, a national park that is on top of a plateau. I went out to the end of the road and hiked over a mile to the very end of the plateau. I struggled the whole time filled with an angst of the ledge giving way or falling somehow, but what nearly inhibited me from taking the next step was the fear of having a seizure, especially in such an isolated place. I stayed as far from the edge as possible until reaching the end of the trail close to the two-thousand-foot ledge. There was a stone to sit on and I crawled up to it because of my fears."

Sara looked away from me as she said, "I can relate to that too."

"It was partly cloudy, so the scenery kept changing as the shadows of the clouds cut off the sunlight and wiped out the colors, accentuating what the sun was able to shine on. For several minutes, I just sat there, scared, but with my mouth hanging open because of what was happening. I felt like a tiny speck in the grand scheme of things, where it makes no difference if I live or die in this world. With everything I'd been through, I felt like nothing. No heart or soul, no one who cared for or loved me. Anything I had or could accomplish would be immediately forgotten. I was insignificant in God's plan. I put my hands over my face and started to cry.

"You see, it was the fear that dominated my life that made me feel that way. For a while I could only focus on the shadows of the clouds, they were like the darkness of a seizure. But after a while I started to notice what was happening as the shadows moved away. That was when the magnificence of the canyon returned, even more amazingly with beautiful colors and shapes. It was even more magnificent after having seen the shadows and the darkness; it was all part of God's plan. It enforced the thought that we should never give up.

"I believed that I'd have control again, and the only way to do so was to continue to push myself into an area where I'm uncomfortable, and to learn how to accept and live with the fear it generates. To accomplish this required more exposure to people and facing my trepidations head on. I was still scared, but eventually I realized my experience could be of help to others dealing with the same issues or loss of hope. Seeing the canyon recover it's magnificent grace made me realize that God is always with us and that such trials make us stronger in the end."

Sara reached out and took my hand, then asked, "Have you ever been back there since then?"

"Yes. A few years ago, I went on another trip to Utah and made it a point to go back to Canyonlands. I walked back to the end of the plateau and sat on the stone at the ledge again, except this time, there was no fear. I had no problem going right up to the edge all along the ridge. I was filled with joy. The joy was through my ability to overcome my fears by understanding how my brain worked and believing in the ability of it to rewire."

I looked right into her sad eyes. "I had the victory of overcoming that fear and achieving what I never thought possible. I know my heart and soul were whole and well. The Lord had been with me the whole time. I was so excited the second time I continued climbing and seeing more of nature's beauty, looking across the canyons from the edge of the ridges.

"During my first visit there was little life in the area due to a prolonged drought. The second time, there had been an unusual rainy season which surrounds me with life, not just near me, but over the thousands of square miles throughout the valley and plateau. I'll definitely be going back again." That was when I felt excited and said, "Would you like to go with me?"

Sara straightened up when she heard the offer, then slouched down with a sad look. "I would love to, but as you well know, travel is a trigger. And being in high places may not be a good thing for me. I'd be so far away from help. What would we do if I needed medical assistance? I guess I'm in the shadow of the clouds right now. My life seems dark in many ways."

A sadness came over me, as I touched her hair and said, "Control will come, and when it does, your world will light up with brighter colors and reopen. All you have to do is believe." Then I squeezed her hand and kissed her on the forehead.

She smiled back and squeezed my hand in return. Thinking of the power of believing made it easy for me to smile at her.

Chapter 27

It took me a moment to assemble my thoughts and share how the doctors told us that everything would improve, and that Sara would be just fine.

It was time for Sara to go with Emily for the week-long seizure monitoring. Her seizures had been limited to arm jerks and seeing multiple items momentarily since she had seen her epileptologist three weeks earlier and was given another antiseizure medication. She told the neurologist assigned to do the testing about the care her neighbor provided and that I had recorded her seizures. She called me as the room was being prepared, then handed the phone to him. For twenty minutes, I described to the neurologist the type of seizures Sara was having. They were very interested in seeing my video recordings and gave me an email address to send it to. They planned to watch it while in the room with Sara as the EEG wiring was attached to her head.

I was surprised when Sara and Emily arrived back at her house a few days early. Sara told me what she could remember, the seizures she had while being monitored and what the doctors recommended. She explained, "As they attached the EEG wires, the seizure alarm went off. I was having a seizure even before the test started and wasn't aware of it. It then progressed and my arm started jerking and I could feel my leg moving. The doctors were watching the whole time, and it was not long after that I could not see or feel anything but could still hear and understand what they were saying. It was terrifying to hear the doctors talk and the critical tone and concern of their statements. I just wish you'd been there. You provide a calming effect in the midst of the storms I face."

I suddenly felt a sense of despair but knew what would have happened to me had I been there, with the likelihood of my traumatic past being reawakened.

I asked Emily about her experience, and she appreciated my openness and knowledge. "Thank you so much for what you do. I never realized the extent of my aunt's seizures and am very grateful for what you are doing. I thought I could handle this as I have a friend with absence seizures, where she stops moving and talking then stares for just a moment. Seeing Aunt Sara's seizures go on for hours and her losing consciousness lasting for so long left me wondering, *Can she die from this?* and *Will she ever get better?*"

Now as we faced the reality of the situation I answered, "Yes, your aunt could die if the seizures continue to progress. However, there is a good possibility she will get better if she wants to and if the doctors find the right medication or combination thereof."

Sara was looking at me with her mouth open and shock written all over her face. I should have been more tactful in addressing Emily's question with Sara hearing me.

Emily continued, "The doctors prescribed another medication to stop Aunt Sara's seizures, so she is now on two anticonvulsant medications for seizures and another for her stroke. This should help tremendously! We were also told she should not live alone because she needs someone to take care of her if the seizures come more often or intensify. She needs to have someone who can be there immediately and to know what to do. I'm scared because I work long hours far away from home, and my husband or I would have to quit work to be her caregiver."

There was some angst in Sara as she responded to the conversation with "Look, this is my house, and I do not want to leave. The doctors promised that eventually everything would improve as they get the right amount of medication in me. I do not want someone living with me now. I recovered from my stroke and can't live with such a setback. Trish can move in for a few days as necessary, and, Matt, you are less than a minute away."

It made sense for me to be Sara's caregiver, especially with my proximity to her house and knowledge of epilepsy. *Was this part of the divine plan to our coming together?* In many ways, I knew that my role was increasing in becoming the caregiver and being called so often. The caring and love we had for one another would have to change if the seizures became the dominant factor between the two of us. She needed the appropriate care to keep her hopeful in finding the right treatment to stop the seizures. All she wanted was to be able to help people as a pastor once again. Hope was what had carried me through my own experience with epilepsy, so it made sense for me to instill hope in Sara to aid in her recovery. My role was changing from being the friend and mentor to becoming the primary caregiver. It seemed simple enough as I was evaluating everything. However, I failed to consider the emotional and mental impact her seizures were having on me.

I went silent as a wave of anxiety began to hit me. I was reliving a cold reality. Carol thought it a good time to end the session, so she came over to me, then turned to the audience, and said, "Be sure to be back tomorrow, Thursday, at ten o'clock, so you can hear what it is like to be a caregiver in similar conditions. I am sure many of you will be able to relate in some way to what is said through your care of someone close to you." She then smiled at me and said, "Call me early tomorrow if you will not be able to make it. I will understand."

There were several people standing near the exit as I was heading to the parking lot. One of them approached me as I came upon them and asked, "Why?" I stopped and looked at them, wondering what they wanted to know with such a general question. They saw the quizzical expression on my face and said, "Why do people like Sara have to suffer so much?" I waited for her colleagues who were now listening before responding. With a serious look she said, "You have used the term *God's plan* a few times, so I am wondering, Why is there any suffering for anyone, especially someone who wants to help so many people?"

I thought for a moment, and suddenly, a scripture I'd read which helped me through recovery came to mind. "Have you ever read any parts of the Bible?" She nodded, so I continued, "In Romans 5:3–4, it says, 'But we also glory in our sufferings, because we know that suffering produces perseverance; perseverance, character; and character, hope.' You see, I once believed we are shaped by what happens in our lives and how we view it all. We may be buried with stress and traumas, but it is our ability to focus on hope that things will change. It's what pulls us through."

Another person then asked, "What happened to your hope for Sara? Seems you had a lot of it, yet it doesn't appear that it came true."

I struggled to respond. "That is what I am searching to find the answer to." I could feel a sense of sadness and doubt trickling through my mind. "That is why I wrote about my experience and I pray the answer will come through sharing it with all of you."

I felt very tired and my mind was shutting down, so it was time to walk away from the group. I sat in my car for quite a while and prayed for an answer that would make sense of the suffering. My emotions ran rampant once more, and although the answer was being given, I just couldn't realize it.

Section IV

Storm Surge

It was shortly after ten o'clock on a Thursday morning. There had to be a day when I was running late. Carol was waiting for me, and seeing me caused her face to light up with a smile, "So glad to see you, seems word has gotten out about your talk. The auditorium is nearly full. Are you ready?" I nodded, and she walked out to the podium to introduce me. She then said, "Mr. Johnson has been talking about someone he met who suffered from a stroke and will be talking about his role as a caregiver today. Please welcome him with a round of applause."

Today was going to be difficult, as I had to face what I'd recently lived through which left me with feelings of defeat, again. Talking to a larger audience made it even more difficult. Carol hadn't dimmed the lights yet, and while I was getting my thoughts together, I saw someone in the center of the room with his hand raised. A technical question might help me with starting because it could create a challenge which often calms down my emotions. I pointed toward the person and said, "I have time for one question. Please tell me your name and your interest in being here."

The person stood up and said, "My name is Gregory Stevens, and I am a psychiatrist here at the hospital. What type of treatment have you been able to obtain to help you through this?"

I looked down at the top of the podium for a moment and then looked back up and said, "I have received much empathy from many people and counselors, but only a few can truly understand the enormity of the experience and what was needed for treatment. Prayer and writing have been effective tools. Writing helped me to understand what actually happened and provided me with a foundation to control my fears and emotions. Talking with people who have lived through similar experiences has been a tremendous help, because they provided an example which proved that recovery is possible. For some reason these people just seem to appear, and you recognize a similarity in their facial expressions, and manner of talk. Sessions are never scheduled; in fact they've all happened with complete strangers. I know this may not be the answer you were looking for as far as your type of work but thank you for asking."

As Greg sat down, he shrugged his shoulders. I saw a look of confusion on his face. I could tell he was looking for information about some miracle medication, but medications only deadened the pain, and they do not resolve the trauma which was experienced.

"Let me continue, and I will tell you about my role as the caregiver. Treatment for caregivers is often overlooked in providing treatment for people dealing with a chronic illness. We tend to focus on the person with the illness and not the trauma the caregivers experience."

I knew this was going to be very difficult as Sara flashed into vision. I was enveloped with sadness, and I was at a momentary loss for words. Several people with tired looks suddenly sat up straighter and learned forward as if this was the most important part of the seminar for them. Seeing them react gave me strength by knowing others were going through similar types of situations. The auditorium then faded away as the lights dimmed, and my thoughts came together and took me back to a very difficult time in my past.

Chapter 28

Sara continued to live alone despite what the epileptologist had said because we lived close together. Her disability limited her options because her pay was reduced and her ability to travel was limited. She enjoyed coming to my house to cook dinner but needed help in the kitchen now. I learned that her seizures had progressed for many days, starting with her left arm jerking for two or three days, resulting in her dropping things. It was not unusual to hear a utensil hit the floor as she momentarily lost control of her left hand. Phone calls to her epileptologist led to increases to her medication to see if it would stop these simple seizures.

I kept sharing my experience which helped her maintain a positive attitude and to endure the nausea often caused by the increase in medication levels. I knew that it could take some time for the body to adapt to the changes in dosage. Even though she did not feel well, she always hugged me and smiled at me, and she talked of how her knowledge of my recovery helped stem her fears of having a seizure. We shared some of the joys we experienced as parents and the associated trials we endured. She was amazed at the accomplishments of my boys, especially with their having to take care of their dad at such young ages. Sara helped me to slow down my busy schedule and take time to reflect and pray.

We were watching a movie after having dinner and sitting on her love seat, when she put her hand in my lap. Without thinking I held it, and it felt much different than when I did so during a seizure. She put her head on my shoulder and I wrapped my arm around her and held her close. The movie was long over before we got up, her loving eyes staring deep into mine as we parted.

At the end of the month, her seizures broke through again and hit both of us hard. It had been affecting a part of her brain for several days, and it smashed through the barrier the medication provided due to her not having slept well for a couple of nights.

Sara had contacted me early in the morning because she had little control of her left arm and it had prevented her from sleeping. A little later, while she was drinking her coffee, it went from the occasional arm jerk to going completely out of control. I was inside my house with the windows open when I thought I heard a scream. "Oh god, make it stop!" My initial reaction was that I'd imagined it. Then my phone message system went off, with Sara's phone number lit up on the display. The message said only: "Help." Samuel was barking consistently.

Rushing over to her house, I found her reclined in her chair. Her left arm was thrashing up and down, and her leg was jerking back and forth. She was semiconscious, half her face distorted as the muscles seized, while the other half was filled with an expression of terror. I saw how she was thrown back into hell with no control and I could only imagine what was racing through her mind as the storm ravaged another part of her brain.

Samuel was running back and forth between the door and Sara, then followed me as I ran over and knelt to be close to her. I took her right hand and assured her she was safe and that I was with her while looking deep into her eyes. As she heard my voice, she started to calm down, yet the turmoil in her brain continued. I will never forget how her face was grossly distorted. I set the timer on my phone and started videotaping part of the seizure for the epileptologist. For eighteen minutes, half her body shook with tremors which had spread into her right side. Throughout all this, she struggled for control while seeking a calm that would stop the horrendous storm going on in her brain. For a moment, she looked like she was going to die as the storm raged mercilessly.

I looked at my phone, it seemed as if the minutes were hours as the battle continued. I fought back my fears and frustration while I forced myself to relate to what she was suffering with. My peripheral vision was gone as I focused completely on Sara's condition. That was when my now deceased grandmother appeared in front of me, screaming as one of my seizures ravaged me on the sofa beside her. Seeing her was like watching an old movie where the characters did not move smoothly as the vision I had flickered on and off and as the seizure spread into the back of my brain where it was processed. There was a raging battling for control as I feared she was having a heart attack from witnessing what was happening to me. This was a vivid memory of what really happened in the past.

This brought up another emotional memory that had been hidden, buried deep in my mind. It was the torment of the seizure, along with rejection from society and the fear of never recovering. I fought that seizure so hard it only caused it to continually intensify. That storm raged for over thirty minutes and left many wounds. The physical ones healed within a few weeks, but the mental ones have never healed, and my self-confidence had been severely damaged. If only I hadn't fought, the storm would have ended sooner.

Suddenly, my grandmother disappeared, and I was brought back to the present day. I looked at the timer. It had been nearly fifteen minutes. What I went through with my seizures tore many of my muscles. How could Sara endure it for nearly twenty minutes? Now I knew what my grandmother had dealt with, as there was nothing I could do for Sara. On the outside, I was calm as I reassured her that I was with her and would not leave, but my brain was in havoc mode with reliving the horror of my past. That's when I realized the importance of telling Sara to quit fighting. "Sara, you're fighting is feeding the seizure, mental calmness is what you need to quiet the storm... stop fighting and search for peace, listen for the voice… Release that tight grip on my hand, hold it like we're on a date… Let the storm blow over and imagine walking along the dock

157

and seeing the sky clear up." Her grip slowly eased, the muscles calmed, and her body quit shaking.

As her ability to see and hear returned, she tried to talk, but I could not understand her because her speech was slurred. Within a few minutes, that part of her brain was no longer affected, and her speech cleared up, and she could tell me of her severe headache and feelings of dread and exhaustion. Samuel was with us the whole time and would not leave until she was able to get off the couch. Samuel and I had a special relationship through our mutual love for Sara. He was aware of her seizures coming and protected her. The only time he would leave her when this happened was to find me.

When she was safe and sleeping to recover from the exhaustion, I called Trish to see if she could come over and stay with Sara for a few days. As I explained what happened, I assured her she would not be alone, and I would be available at any time if needed. Trish seemed like an angel, as she was always available and said she would be over in a couple of hours.

For my own peace of mind, I called Jennifer to tell her what was witnessed. I told her about Sara's seizure and seeing our grandmother sitting across from me, screaming for help. It was nice to have someone to process this with as I realized the flashback was an indicator of PTSD. Jennifer gave me a sense of relief by just listening and assuring me she would always be available to help. She brought me back to reality when she asked, "Is providing care for Sara healthy for you?"

I responded, "It seems as though I'm supposed to be here, like some form of spiritual calling. My recall helped in treating Sara and pulling her out of the seizure. I'd be abandoning the person if I ignored her calls or refused to help. Aren't we supposed to reach out to those in need? I'd be a total failure since my work and experience is what this person needs." After we hung up the phone, I prayed and asked God to stop Sara's seizures, to heal her and make her whole again.

The next day, Sara told me how she was overwhelmed with fear as she lost control of her body, then fought for control. She explained, "I wanted it to stop as I felt thrown into a fight that filled me with a sense of dread. I knew I was safe when I heard your voice, even more so when I felt your hand holding mine. It was my lifeline, and what you said enabled me to quit fighting, and now I have access to recovery and peace."

Full recovery, including from the headache took several more days. Based on my experience, I shared how recovery from the injury, tiredness, and getting the mind to reset took several days. She was appreciative of my openness, but something was different this time. I had seen many people have seizures, but I have never had such an emotional reaction as when I watched Sara have one.

Dr. Leyde would not talk to me without Sara on the phone, and it would take a couple of days before she recovered enough to make the call. She was told to increase her medication dosage, and the doctor, knowing of my experience, was pleased to know of my availability in being her caregiver. "It is important that Sara not live alone. We need to get control of these seizures, and as you know, Matt, she cannot do this by herself. Furthermore, I do not want her to drive until I see her again in a few weeks."

I felt overwhelmed. With Sara being a pastor, she could not be dependent on her congregation for housing and all her transportation needs because they could not afford it. She never had time to make friends with other people in the area besides myself and was further limited in that by her seizures. I'd also experienced the isolation and severe depression caused by the driving restrictions that were once placed on me. I did not want Sara to suffer what I had to endure. Then I thought about being her driver again and felt an even tighter level of restriction on myself. I should have remembered that Trish was available to help too.

Our relationship was changing. Trish had seen one of Sara's seizures and said she could not watch her have another. She was willing to stay with Sara as long as she could call on me if a seizure was to occur. All three of us prayed that Sara would regain control of her seizures soon. It would be just over three weeks until the next appointment with the epileptologist, and I knew it would take some time to implement any new medications. Sara quickly realized the burden she was placing on us and told me how this tore at her self-esteem.

Driving to see her epileptologist took several hours and several more to return home. It made for a long day, particularly with the stress caused by seeing a doctor about a condition that compromises a person's ability to function and associate with others. A person may be whole and functional most of the time, but the few minutes of a seizure and the accompanying stigmas become the lock and chain that restricts their ability to live.

Dr. Leyde once again explained the laws in the state associated with driving after having been and being treated for seizures. Fortunately, the law was written only as a recommendation to the doctors and client and not a mandate. He wanted to verify that Sara had a warning to her seizure coming through the jerking of her left hand long before it impacted her cognitive senses and ability to drive. Once we confirmed this, he reiterated she was restricted to driving locally, and not in any city setting or within twenty-four hours of her arm jerking.

We were both relieved as Sara now had her freedom to drive back and I had the freedom to focus caring for myself. After my own past experiences, I was afraid we would be told she would not be allowed to drive; it seemed that I would have to relive the dependency such restrictions placed on me. I felt guilty when I was not available to help because I felt a need to pay back those who had helped me many years earlier. My sleep was affected because I had to watch what I'd dreaded most of my life coming true, only in someone else.

When possible, we still enjoyed each other's company and had fun preparing dinner and eating together. We enjoyed taking Samuel for walks in the neighborhood and talking about working together someday. Going downtown to the waterfront to visit and see all the boats and talk to the owners and visitors was fulfilling.

It was on one of these walks that Sara told me more about her experience during the EEG monitoring. "As you know, I can still hear during a seizure, and heard a voice I thought was the doctor. Emily said there was no one in the room at the time."

"What did you hear?" I asked.

"It was a woman's voice, very calming and assuring." She said, then continued with, "You've done well and I am with you."

We had a lot to be thankful full for this Thanksgiving.

Chapter 29

As Christmas was approaching, Sara shared more about her having epilepsy with the church board. It brought a sense of relief and reduced the stress as most members were very helpful and provided all kinds of support to help get through celebrating Christmas. For Sara, the reduced responsibility and support from the board members helped immensely. However, she continued to struggle with assembling the sermons and during the service had to have someone else handle the congregation's financial gifts. They had to be ready to do the scripture readings because her eyes began to wander more often. Even with the support, we had a very tough Christmas filled with simple partial seizures.

With the stress of Christmas being over and the support the church members provided, it seemed she could relax and recover. With less stress and responsibility, the seizures were minor in nature for many weeks. With control regained, we visited some of the places in the region we had talked of and, most importantly, went sailing again. To improve her stamina, she had been going to the gym for nearly a month, and her health seemed to be improving.

It seemed we finally had the right medication and dosage to control her seizures, and my fear of her having one subsided. We talked more about working together in various ministries through her church and community. She had been doing so well we even talked about ministering to other people recovering from strokes and epilepsy. It seemed like God had a plan for the two of us, only in our case it included a medical setting. Trish appreciated that she was no longer needed, however, appreciated may be the wrong word; rather it should be that she was relieved from the high level of responsibility she carried.

We were feeling very positive about our future. We were sitting next to each other watching a program at her house when I placed my hand on her lap. The roles were reversed this time, as she put her arm over my shoulder and pulled me into her. To be held is important for everyone and was exactly what I needed after all the responsibility, worry, and flashbacks which occurred that were triggered by her seizures. The role of the pastor in her came through, the part of Sara that I admired and prayed would return. Maybe "pastor" is the wrong term, as it's more essential to be held by someone who loves you. She held me for a long time after turning off the TV, it was late in the evening before my going home.

The next day a phone call from the hospital came about Jennifer. Earlier in the day, she had fallen off her horse and had been admitted. Her lower back was broken in several places, and she possibly could never ride again. When Sara heard about what had happened, she assured me she was fine and told me to get to the hospital. She would call Trish if needed. I raced to the hospital where Jennifer was in the emergency room. The good news was she still had feeling and the ability to move her legs; however, several of her lower vertebrae were shattered. Major surgery was required to relieve her pain and enable her to walk once again.

Visiting Jennifer was difficult as she struggled with the pain and fear of never being able to ride again, something she loved to do since childhood. She was in the hospital for several days in an area adjacent to the neurological section. I stayed with her until her daughter arrived the next day and then visited them every day. Not once did I have any flashbacks of being in the hospital having surgery, experienced when visiting Sara. Jennifer was very pleased I could help.

I moved into Jennifer's house when she came home so I could be her caregiver for a few weeks. She required help getting out of bed in the morning and down to the main level of her house. After breakfast and feeding her pets, I would return home to check on Sara. She continued to do well, and Jennifer had a remarkable comeback, as she could walk and was able to take care of herself in remarkable time.

Spring came very early, and Sara tried to plan for Easter, with Ash Wednesday still several weeks away. It was a Sunday morning and Sara had done well getting dressed and was ready to go to the church. She had slept too, seemed very happy, and joked about how her mind was now working, something only those of us with brain injury would find funny. The first service went well, and she was almost beaming with delight, having done the entire service without help. But there was something about the second service that triggered her seizures. Just before the seizure started, I noticed her arm jerk and her smile disappeared.

Once again, the she lost control of her arm while presenting the offerings. She was ready and nothing spilled, but the seizure did not stop there, it spread as she turned to face the congregation and her leg went out from under her. With her arm not being functional and her leg gone she fell hard. Running up to her I saw her face was half distorted, the seizure storm was underway, affecting not just Sara, but the whole congregation. The choir was the closest to her and quickly gathered round, their robes creating a wall blocking the view of the congregation.

I sat on the floor to protect Sara's head in my lap. She took hold of my left hand and squeezed it, her way of acknowledging my presence. I expressed appreciation of the choir's concern and told them if they could not bear to watch what was happening to turn around, their robes providing the privacy needed. Now, it was time to pray, and the choir director was asked to lead the congregation in prayer. Hearing this, the terror on Sara's face went away, and I reminded her not to battle with the seizure. She was safe physically and emotionally, and like with me, the calmness shortened the time of the seizure, and a few minutes later her left side stopped shaking and she slipped into an exhaustive sleep.

Several people helped in getting her to the couch in her office and Tracy stayed with her. It seemed that half the congregation was still in the church, along with most of the choir. Everyone looking for answers. The choir sat in the pews as I went up to the front, and it was time to address the fear and unknowns of epilepsy. It would take nearly two hours to explain and answer the many questions that were asked, the ones I could not answer were associated with whether this would ever happen again. Everyone was reassured Sara would be fine in a few hours, however, I didn't realize the amount of blood I had on my shirt from her chewing on her tongue and lip.

That evening Sara's world would be turned upside down, as Craig, the church director, came to her house to tell her the news. We were about to learn that soon after I took her home an emergency meeting was held by him with his board members and they decided that Sara could no longer be a part of the church. Apparently, there were many phone calls that afternoon exchanged amongst the church members because what had happened scared many, several were going to leave the church unless something happened soon. Sara had done well to hold herself together, especially with the headache she experienced and now she received this slap in the face. She was expressionless and made no response, and she just sat quietly, in shock.

That I was upset is a mild way of expressing what my reaction was at that time. Craig was not happy, he really did like Sara, but this was all that he and his staff could think of to remedy the situation. Seeing that Sara was quiet, I asked, "What about giving Sara some time to find the proper treatment for the seizures and her returning in say, three months?"

Craig looked at me, and smiled, "I think that could happen. We've had pastors go on sabbaticals for a few months, and we replace them temporarily. I really like this idea. Do you think her seizures can be treated by then? Three months is about as long as we can allow."

"I guess if it's going to happen it will happen. When will you be able to confirm if this will be okay?"

Craig grinned and said, "Right now, my position gives me such authority." The life instantly returned to Sara face, and she almost smiled, then quietly said, "Thank you."

Knowing the intensity of her headache I told Craig, "She probably won't be able to say much more, because of the injuries from earlier today, but thank you for your consideration and allowing time to get her seizures controlled. This will also reduce her stress for a while which is a major trigger to the seizures.

Craig promised to handle everything with the church so Sara could stay home and focus on getting the right treatment. An incredible amount of effort would be required, not only with finding the right medications but she would also be going through a battle of survival in her mind in a compressed amount of time.

Chapter 30

To help me recover and bring us peace of mind, Sara thought it best to get away and spend a day sailing. This always brought her a sense of joy and fullness, too. We had a favorite place, a little cove a few hours sail away that was off the intracoastal waterway. The cove provided a sense of safety from the elements, the water was calm, and the breeze always felt good. Sailing seemed a good way to treat our anxiety and depression, which are both triggers to seizures.

When it was warmer, we could swim in clean, clear water and enjoy watching the dolphins. Sara felt so good, doing what she loved the most, that it caused her to forget about her health and job. She became filled with joy and laughter—something she had not experienced for many months. For both of us, the past was forgotten, and the future was put on hold. We were in the present moment, enriched with the natural beauty that surrounded us.

After lunch, Sara took a nap. When she woke up, she looked very pale and asked if we could sail home soon. "I cannot put it into words, but something is happening in my head. I feel very anxious and scared, and now there are two of you looking at me. I've gotten up four times, but in actuality, only got up once." I could see her right-hand twitching and her eyes wandering. She returned to a berth, and I immediately got the boat underway.

It is amazing how one's mind can feed into the feeling of terror by imagining the many different scenarios of what could happen; these "what-if" questions were racing through my mind as I started the engine and worked hard to get the anchor raised. What if Sara had a full complex seizure? What if I couldn't get her to emergency care right away? What if the boat broke down? It would take the coast guard or police several hours to get to us by boat, and a helicopter rescue could be very dangerous.

It would be quicker to get the boat under sail, but that would prevent me from responding to Sara if she had a full seizure. It had been about an hour when Sara emerged all of a sudden from below, and said, "I'm feeling better now. My arm has stopped twitching, and my head is clear. I'm sorry about needing to get back home early."

I noticed she seemed to be hanging on tight and swaying a little out of time with the motion of the boat, and so I asked, "Are you feeling well enough to help so we can get under sail? The wind is favorable, and we can get home sooner."

A look of excitement came over her. "I'll go forward and raise the mainsail. It feels good to be out of the cabin now."

She jumped up and quickly stepped out of the cockpit and ran to the foredeck. I was surprised with her action because she should have stayed within the safety of the cockpit and taken the wheel from me. I started to say something, but she didn't listen as she untied the halyard to the mainsail. She pulled the sail up quickly, and everything seemed to be going well as the wind filled the sail and the boat heeled slightly. The boat became much quieter as I shut down the engine and, for a moment, we were filled with peace. It had taken me several minutes to do everything needed with the sail trim before noticing it was taking Sara a long time to finish tying the cleat hitch and coiling the halyard. Ordinarily this would have been completed in a minute, yet she still stood at the base of the mast, working and working at tying a simple knot. Then she looked up at me with anger lines streaming all over her face as she screamed, "I can't even tie a damn cleat!"

I put the boat on autopilot and climbed forward to help her. After securing the halyard, I assured her the setback was only momentary and she would get better soon.

On her way back to the cockpit, she fell hard and rolled toward the side of the boat. As she was about to fall overboard, she grabbed one of the stanchions, giving me time to grab hold of her and prevent her from falling off. My heart was racing while helping her to recover to a kneeling position. Slowly, she crawled back to the cockpit and sat on the seat, sweating profusely and in pain from the bruises on her arms and legs. I checked her over to make sure she was safe, then noticed the twitching of her arm had returned. She went silent and stared at the deck. To get the boat moving faster, I got the jib sail unfurled and trimmed. The boat was now making good time, and the GPS indicated we were twenty miles from the dock and the safety of home.

Sara looked up at me and saw my expression of concern for her and the lines of fear created by the situation. A sadness engulfed her. "Sailing used to give me a peace of mind, but now I'm really scared." I put my arm around her and gave her a long hug. Eventually, she pushed me away and said, "You need to concentrate on sailing the boat. I'm okay now," as she wiped her face dry. For the next hour, she just sat in the cockpit, staring over the side of the boat, listening to the wind and the boat cutting through the water.

It was past dinner time, and we still had a couple of hours to sail. I tried to regain a positive attitude by asking her, "I can make some sandwiches for dinner if you can take the helm, or should I activate the autopilot?"

A smile returned to her face as she responded, "I can take the wheel now. I'm doing much better again. It should help me to concentrate on something I've always loved to do."

As she got into position behind the wheel, she winced after bumping her leg and hitting one of the many bruises from her earlier fall. Her smile immediately returned when she took the wheel and became the captain of the boat. Seeing her back to her old self brought me a sense of relief, so I went below to the galley and started making sandwiches.

It had only been a few minutes when I noticed the boat was not moving and the sails were flapping in the wind. I looked up and saw Sara turning the wheel back and forth. Initially, I thought she was joking with me, and then saw the frustration in her face again. She was angry, then she saw me come on deck and said, "I can't even remember which way to turn the wheel!" Not only was her left arm jerking slightly now, but her leg began to shake too.

"No problem, I've got it," I said in a calming tone, then taking the wheel and getting the boat back on course. I put my arm around her and shut down my own emotions to keep from weeping. I stayed in the cockpit and could not make dinner, and neither could she. Although I could sail the boat all by myself, I was filled with doubt and kept telling myself, "There's no way to sail while taking care of Sara."

Sara had to move to a safe place, out of my way, leaving me very nervous about her state of mind and my own. Getting the boat safely back to the dock was easy with two people as it was necessary to simultaneously steer, drop sail, and tie-off the boat to the pilings at the dock. I handled everything alone, getting the boat under engine power, then dropping the sails. The wind was favorable, and the boat came to a stop just a couple feet from the dock as we came into the slip and a stern line was attached. Sara was impressed with my ability but was sad as she no longer felt like part of the crew.

With the boat at the dock, she tried to help with putting the equipment away. As she started to go below to stow the handles to the winches, she stopped and said, "I cannot remember where these go," as she stared at them.

I was tying off the bow lines and looked over my shoulder while replying, "Your kidding, right? You have put them away many times. They go on the shelf on the starboard side."

She kept staring at the handles. "Which side is starboard?" The serious look she had at the tools left me no doubt that truly she could not remember.

After securing the lines, I walked back to the cockpit. Sara was still standing at the stairway as I came up to her; she just kept staring at the handles, wondering where they were to be stored. I tapped her on her shoulder, and she turned around and gave them to me. "Why don't you come up and take a seat by the wheel? I'll take care of the boat," I said. After she sat down, she kept staring at her hands.

It was difficult getting her off the boat and onto the dock as her left arm and leg continued to twitch every few minutes. Any future sailing with her was now in doubt. Physical injury was very probable as she had fallen several times and had many bad bruises. I could not imagine how I would have gotten her back on the boat had she fallen overboard. Although she was an excellent swimmer, would she have been able to swim if she was unable to use her left arm or leg? Sara was afraid of what might have happened while on the boat and how this fear fed a seizure. As we walked down the dock to the car, I wondered, *Was she dragging her leg because of an issue with her nerves, or was it caused by the heavy chain of disability she was trapped in?*

Her enthusiasm was gone as she returned to the reality of losing her job permanently and living with epilepsy. As we drove home, I felt defeated and quietly asked myself, *Would the person I've cared for ever fully recover?* Our trips on the boat were now over; our dream trip to the barrier islands together was just that—a dream.

Chapter 31

Although Sara had not lost consciousness with the seizures while sailing, she was struggling with the depression caused by fearing the loss of her job, and not being able to sail, at least for a while. Fortunately, her memory had recovered, although there were parts of the sailing trip she could not recall. The gym was now her haven and she texted me that she was on her way there. She looked forward to our going on a walk downtown and having dinner together later in the day. It did not seem long after receiving her text when my phone rang, with her name on the screen.

I answered with "Good morning, Sara!" then heard a man's voice as he replied, "This is Michael, with the gym staff. Is this Sara's friend Matt?" I confirmed it was, and he said in an anxious voice, "Sara has you down as her emergency point of contact. She was able to call you but lost her ability to speak when you answered. She's having a seizure. Can you help us?" He then told me how the staff reacted by moving her into a room where none of their other clients could see what was happening.

I felt a surge of uneasiness as Michael told me the details of what happened. "She had started some weightlifting and suddenly let go of the machine, making a loud crashing sound. I saw her get up; her left arm was jerking as she shouted for help. A staff member got to her quickly and helped her into a small room as her legs gave way. I was with her within a minute and she handed me her phone because she could not talk, her face then became distorted. The seizure is continuing, and we need to know if we should call 911. Her seizure was longer than five minutes, and we were taught to do so when this happens in training." I informed him that her seizures last up to twenty minutes and according to the doctor, that calling emergency services would not be necessary unless she was injured.

He seemed relieved when I said, "I am on my way and should be there in a few minutes."

He thanked me, and I heard him tell someone, "Do not call for the ambulance. Her friend Matt will be here soon."

Although I felt the urge to race to the gym, I had to remind myself it was not necessary. She was in a safe place with a group of medical staff located next to a hospital. When I arrived, she was doing better. She was conscious and able to talk a little.

She smiled when she saw me; however, it was not a complete smile because she had not fully recovered from the seizure. She was in a wheelchair, and I assumed her leg was still affected, then noticed a slight twitching in her left arm and hand. The smile was the most important indicator that confirmed she was in the recovery stage of the seizure. Michael was with her and seeing her face light up with a smile as I approached, realized I was the person he talked to on the phone. He smiled while holding out his hand as he introduced himself.

I smiled at both and shook Michael's hand and then held Sara's. Michael looked a little pale, so I said, "I see Sara's coming back," then felt her hand squeeze mine in a loving way. "How are you and the staff doing? Did any of your customers see what happened?"

"There are some of us who are a little shaken. We studied about seizures in school and saw some videos, but this is the first time any of us actually witnessed one. Sara was good in letting us know the seizure was coming as her legs were shaking."

My eyebrows went up when he said *legs*. "I am glad she had some privacy with this. You said *legs*. That is odd because it usually only affects her left side."

Michael explained, "It started in her left arm, then into the left leg and face. About ten minutes later, her right leg began to shake too."

As he was telling me this, I felt a sense of frustration as the seizures seem to be getting more complex and now affected both sides of her brain. The sense of fighting so hard and yet suffering such a setback was what I was mad about. Once again, I was reminded to persevere as I saw the message on the sleeve of my Army running shirt which said, "Never Quit."

I knelt down to talk face to face with Sara as she quietly said, "I'm so embarrassed. Can we leave now?"

I smiled and assured her it was time to go. We needed help getting her into my car, but when we got to her home, she could use her leg again and was able to walk into her house. She got into her favorite chair, and I covered her with a blanket. Samuel came up to be with her. As I leaned over to give her a kiss, she wrapped her arms around me and hugged me like never before, then we both broke down and cried. I kissed her again as I pulled myself away and said, "Never quit." She smiled and replied, "I never will." We still had forty days to get total control before she would lose her job.

As Sara rubbed Samuel's ear, she assured me it was safe to leave her alone and return to the gym to get her car, so I called Jennifer to give me a ride. As we rode back to the gym, Jennifer wanted to know everything that happened. When I finished telling her, she said, "You didn't say anything about what happened to you, and that is what I need to hear about."

"I'm fine."

"Then why were your eyes so red when you got into my car? I take it you've been crying."

"I can't hide anything from you, sister. You are right. We both have been crying. It just totally sucks to watch someone you love suffer from a seizure." A moment later I shouted, "Damn it!" in frustration.

She gave me that surprised look and said, "This must really be hard on you. I never hear you swear!" We were both quiet for a moment, then she followed up with "So now you know how I felt when I watched my little brother have a grand mal seizure in my house several years ago."

"Sorry about that. But that was just one time. I have seen Sara have nearly a dozen, and it just gets harder with each one. They are getting more intense too."

As we pulled up next to Sara's car, Jennifer said, "Take care of yourself, brother. This seems to be taking more out of you each time it happens."

"I just love her more than I thought, and that makes it harder and harder to live with. Thanks, sister. I'll keep in touch. Love you."

She gave me a serious look and said, "Love you too, brother. You can still have seizures, and I'm concerned about the stress Sara's condition is creating for you. You have to call me when you get home."

Jennifer's remark about stress reminded me of how pale Michael looked when I came to get Sara at the gym and thought it best to go over and talk to the staff. Michael looked much better as I approached him this time. He had some of the staff join us upon learning my reason for coming back. We talked about what they saw and, most importantly, what they had felt while watching Sara's seizure. All responded about having some level of fear as they witnessed what was happening to her. We then talked about the stages of a seizure, Sara's ability to hear, and the appropriate response in her case. It was most important to get support from others, something I desperately needed for myself, but thought I was strong enough to be without it. I shared some of my own experience of living with seizures and as a mentor I answered the questions about my source of knowledge. I then asked them, "Is it okay for Sara to come back to use the gym in a few days?" I was assured that this would be fine, especially now that they knew what to do and could call me if something happened.

My experience taking seizure medications and surviving breakthrough seizures brought Sara hope, but did not eliminate her fears. She was scared about having another one and agreed to call Dr. Leyde. We had difficulty getting an appointment because she was always very busy. The medical staff were terrific once they understood the necessity of Sara getting control for her continuing to work as a pastor. Her appointment was moved up a few weeks as Dr. Leyde made time to see her.

It took over a week for Sara's muscles to heal from the damage that occurred during the seizure, and for her to get over her feelings of embarrassment before she returned to the gym. To help the staff, she gave them a copy of a book about living with epilepsy and being a caregiver. The staff was very appreciative, and the nurses and trainers were able to learn more about seizures and how to respond to them. It was all good now that everyone had inside information about epilepsy as Sara's seizures were coming more often. For Sara, this provided a level of comfort knowing the staff would be ready to help her.

Chapter 32

My property and house were my safe haven that enabled me to recover from watching Sara have a seizure. The safest areas were the workshop and yard because Sara did not visit me there, as this mostly took place in the house. She realized how important it was for me to have my own space. The yard enabled me to be outdoors, as I planted and tended to a garden and reestablished a beautiful flower bed. By the middle of the summer, there were the tomatoes, zucchini, and cucumbers, along with canning and pickling many more to have into the winter. The flower beds were best in the Spring and Fall.

I used the workshop during the rainy days and colder months. The lathe was what I enjoyed the most and I started to learn how to make dowels and finished furniture. I made pens out of wood from the communities nearby and the hardwoods saved from Jennifer's property. A friend was opening a new store in the historic district, and gave me some of the old wood flooring and I made pens that were special as he told customers, "This came from the original flooring used in this building when it was built in 1890."

Sara said she needed some bookshelves to organize some of the textbooks from her studies as a tool to help her memory recover. We talked of the benefits as this was a way to organize her office and have easy access to important information. I knew this was critical because she would soon forget what she needed or was trying to find. For me, it would be a healthy challenge to accomplish something requiring my own special skills and abilities, which boosted my self-esteem.

We talked of what was needed, and I drew a sketch of a desk and a set of bookshelves; she offered some good advice on the finishes. It took many hours, and I felt great knowing I was able to help her beyond the role of being her caregiver. Sara began to beam as the bookshelf was installed in her house, and she found a sense of peace not found for many months.

My hopes were revived as I watched how well she organized everything. She had boxes and boxes of books and sorted them by subject matter and space needed. It would take several days, yet it was an indication her mind was coming back together. She would pull a book down and, without opening it, explain the subject matter and why it should be read. I was listening to a pastor once again and was excited for her. For days, she told me how pleased she was with her new office and her ability to pull information from her books, which she had limited access to earlier.

It was a week after she finished getting her office established, when she came over to my house to fix lunch for both of us. I was finishing some work in the yard when there was a loud knock on the window and I saw Sara waving at me. Samuel was with her, barking until he saw me running into the house. The fear that she was having another seizure gripped my mind as I leapt up the steps on the deck and rushed into the house. Much to my surprise Sara was in the kitchen serving lunch and singing to herself. She was surprised to see me standing near the entry, breathing hard with my face loaded with concern that I would find her having a seizure. Suffice to say it took some time before my appetite returned and we could have a quiet lunch together.

Chapter 33

My experience with Sara's seizures helped me understand the stress my family endured watching me have seizures. I remembered the battles we fought, with the struggle to maintain some form of hope and the threatening demise of my character in the darkest times. Now I was living the experience of the caregiver. Thinking about Sara's experience with the stroke, I wondered, *How could God let people who have suffered so much suffer even more?*

When we saw Dr. Leyde, I asked, "What should be the proper dosage of her medication? Too high and she has simple partial seizures triggered by the toxicity. Too low and she has full complex seizures. Isn't there another medication we can use?"

Dr. Leyde looked at me with a very serious expression and replied, "Look, as you know, there are several different medications we can use, but she is already on three. We could try another medication, but many people cannot afford it, and knowing Sara's current work situation, there is no way she can. I also don't want to see the rest of her body damaged by the side effects. There is another readily available, however it often impacts a person's memory and although it stops the seizures, it alters their personality. We need to try one that is used when she has a seizure. It is the emergency pill, and you slip it under her tongue as she feels the seizure coming. If she does not get it in time, it will be ineffective to prevent the seizure from spreading."

The risk of a seizure coming increased because she no longer had prolonged hours of warning by her arm twitching. The seizures would progress within a few minutes or even a few seconds of the warning symptoms now.

We still felt some relief knowing there was another treatment available. Sara did well for another week, and we decided to drive her car to a nearby store where we could shop for badly needed clothes. She was excited about driving and relieved I would accompany her. As we approached the mall, she suddenly pulled into a parking lot. I initially thought she had made a wrong turn until seeing her arm jerk. She didn't say anything and pointed toward the glove compartment. Inside was a small bottle of the emergency medication. I put a pill in her right hand, and she dropped it as she tried to get it to her mouth. I got another and managed to get it into her mouth. In this short time period, the seizure had already spread and affected nearly a third of her body, but within seconds of taking the pill the symptoms subsided and her body began to calm down. Her face returned to normal, and she was responsive and in control. A few minutes later, she moved over to the passenger seat, and I drove us home. She did not look at me the whole way as she sat with her head back, recovering from the headache she talked about, but not from the feelings of defeat as was evident in her expression. I was relieved knowing she had the ability to pull off the road and had the emergency medication with her.

We needed to establish a system that would allow people to know where the emergency medication was and for her to have access to it with just her right hand. This was important because it was less than a week later when Sara was working out at the gym and felt a seizure coming. She was able to get her emergency medication in her mouth, and it stopped. However, the medication removed her ability to stay awake, and the staff called me to take her home. I was thankful that the medication worked but fearful that she was not able to take it in time in the future. She was now having two to three simple seizures and one complex seizure a week.

On several occasions, she had the pill bottle in her right hand as a seizure progressed into a complex partial seizure. She could not open the bottle because she no longer had control of her left hand. Other times, she had simply forgotten about her emergency medication, even though she had it in her pocket. I was always notified of the seizures occurring but could not always be in time to assist with administering the emergency medication. Witnessing these most advanced seizures take place with her now caused mine to return, either as an aura, a flashback, or both. We were out of options as far as medications and the only option was to trace the triggers causing them, our conclusions came as quite a surprise.

Chapter 34

Sara's epileptologist had increased her level of medication a number of times, and the side effects were magnified whenever she took them in the morning. The side effects were the same as the pre-ictal stage of her seizures; dizziness, seeing multiple images, and her arm jerking. I got so frustrated and concerned one day that I made her go to the hospital. We were both relieved when she was not admitted, but blood samples were taken to determine her medication levels. Over the next several days, the same thing happened, with seizure-like symptoms occurring soon after she took her morning medication.

I was aware of what was happening as I had been through the same situation when my body could no longer process my medication fast enough. When the body cannot filter out the amount taken by the time another dose is consumed, the level in the blood continues to increase. After days or weeks, the medication becomes toxic, and taking another dose increases it three to five times. In my case, the high toxicity resulted in the loss of balance and the ability to take care of my two sons, who were young and deeply affected by their father's disability.

With Sara, the seizures horrified her to the point she was scared to skip a dose. It would take a few days to get the test results back, and we would find that indeed, her medication had gone toxic. What was supposed to help her was doing harm to her organs and severely impacting sections of her brain. This explained what had happened on the boat and her difficulty remembering the basic necessities—of where the boat equipment was stored or how to tie a knot. Even cleaning up the kitchen was now a challenge, something she had never had problems with before. My stress level significantly increased because Jennifer, with her back injury, would no longer able to support me if Sara was lost to another seizure.

It had been two weeks since Sara's medication was reduced, and she recovered well; her memory and balance had improved significantly, and she seemed fully functional once more. Soon after her abilities returned, she wanted to come over to my house and make dinner as a way to repay me for all my time and assistance. I appreciated this as I was behind schedule on my house renovations. While cleaning up part of yard, there came a loud pounding noise from the porch room. I looked over and saw Sara in the window. When she had my attention, she ran back into the living room and collapsed as the left side of her body was seizing and she fell onto the couch. Thinking dinner was ready, I walked back into the house. Seeing she was not in the kitchen, I rushed into the living room, where she was on the couch and had slipped into a complex partial seizure.

Kneeling on the floor beside her, I picked up her right hand and calmly said, "I'm here with you, and you're going to be fine."

She could hear me, and the right side of her body relaxed once again as the tension subsided. She knew she was safe. Then her whole face became distorted as the seizure continued to spread into the right half of her body, then her whole body seized. She could no longer hold my hand.

I repeatedly said, "I will always be with you," as I watched and felt her entire body jerk in convulsions. I tried to mentally survive the moment by approaching the situation from a mentor perspective in order to maintain control of the emotional part of my brain. It was difficult to witness the distortion of her face, especially for so long.

I had become so involved in her seizure that it triggered my own. An aura began as I looked her distorted face and felt the seizure through her right arm. Once again, that familiar nauseous sensation filled my shoulders and moved into my stomach while my heart raced. I was suddenly filled with fear as my brain's center of emotions was overwhelmed by the seizure. In order to stop it I had to analyze what had triggered it, but this method did not work because the answer was so obvious since it was in front of me—Sara's seizure. My seizure lasted longer than usual, and for a moment, I thought I was going to slip into a grand mal seizure myself. Then the nausea went away, but my heart rate did not slow down.

An impenetrable amount of fear was left in me—fear of Sara's seizure and my own. As my system recovered, Sara started to come out of her seizure. I wondered if the first thing she saw was my pale face for she reached up to touch my cheek. I felt terrible about her situation and how her seizures were affecting me and my memories.

I said, "Welcome back. You are safe, and I'll always be with you, no matter what," with a little more emphasis on the last part. As the distortion of her face faded, she was still pale and covered in sweat. Her eyes kept wandering out of synchronization, indicating the seizure was still ongoing in part of her brain. It took several more minutes for this to stop, and she was able to focus on me. A slightly distorted smile formed on her lips. It would be another few minutes before she could speak, and her first words were, "Are you okay? My god, my head hurts." I assured her I was fine and excused myself to get us both something to drink.

While in the kitchen, I thought of what she saw when she was recovering, and suddenly the kitchen was gone and I was laying on the floor somewhere, watching my son talking to some paramedics during a time I was having a grand mal seizure. To pull myself back to reality, I quickly opened a cabinet to force a change to the setting, and the flashback went away. I grabbed some glasses and got both of us some ice-cold water.

When I was back with Sara, I helped her sit up, and she appreciated a few sips of the cool water. I noticed she was covered in sweat as I told her, "I'll be back in a minute. Let me get you a cool towel."

I went into the bathroom, and while soaking a small towel with cold water, saw myself in the mirror. I understood why she asked me if I was okay. My complexion was very pale, indicating a form of shock. I was buried in despair. Once again, I had to pull myself together to be presentable to her. Several deep breaths helped me control my emotions. As she saw me returning, I smiled and continued with welcoming her back from the seizure. She greatly appreciated the coolness of the damp towel as I wiped her face and neck. I never told her that it had many tears on it too.

She later told me she was demanding too much and apologized for what was happening. We were no longer able to take any trips together without the threat of a seizure and were feeling isolated. At least she had me to help her. I was on my own because she could not take the pressure of worrying about my health without her seizures becoming more intense, and she was already filled with guilt about the demands of her poor health. We agreed the next time she came over to bring Samuel with her. He had a way of comforting both of us.

With her having such a complex seizure in my house, I could no longer go into a room without thinking about her. My safe zone was intruded upon yet being together with her was comforting for me as she always gave me a hug and made me feel better about myself. Her house, and now mine, were mentally damaging for both of us—and it was beyond repair.

My survival required me getting away from the pressure caused by worry, the type that depresses a person and is detrimental to their health. Sara's seizures were under control again with a slight increase in her medications and she recognized my depression and hoped that a trip away from the area would provide me some peace. She told me, "Please go sailing for a few days. I'm doing okay now and am very worried about you. Trish or Jennifer can get me to the hospital if something were to happen. I love you, and it hurts to see you like this." I agreed to go and felt a sense of relief as I got ready.

Chapter 35

It was time to explain more of the mental and physical battles I faced due to the stress Sara's seizures were creating in me. If only we had been established in the community and had friends who we could call on throughout all this.

Being away from Sara and home seemed a good way to recharge my body and mind, especially being alone on my sailboat where I always felt the spiritual presence of God. Although we had a storm a few weeks earlier that caused some flooding and debris to be swept into the river, it all should have cleared up by now. The weather was perfect for a three-day sail with lots of sunshine, warm temperatures, moderate winds, and possibly a few thunderstorms. I was well-prepared and felt very confident making the trip all by myself. Little did I know that my sailing ability would be tested to the extreme. When Sara saw me come into my house the Sunday evening after the trip, she came over and greeted me with a smile that quickly turned into an expression of concern. I was pale and looked exhausted, so she asked, "What happened?"

I started to tell her how I thought the debris from the flooding would have been out of the river by now. My trip down the river to an anchorage along the intracoastal waterway started three days ago. She cut me off by saying "Matt, I already know this. Why are you telling me again?"

It was because my mind was confused by the auras that I had that day and forgot I had shared this plan with her the night before I left. I wasn't able to fully understand her question, so I continued, "It was approaching sunset, and the wind was calming down. So, I started the engine and increased speed to be able to anchor before it was totally dark. The boat felt good with the light wind and momentum of the engine."

I smiled at her, then explained how the boat was moving along at six knots, her maximum speed, when suddenly, it slammed to a stop and started to climb out of the water. "It was as though a giant sea monster had grabbed the boat from below and was trying to topple her over backward. I held on tight to keep from falling and saw the head of the monster come surging out of the water on my left. For a moment, I thought it really was some satanic creature coming for me."

She asked, "What was it?"

My expression became serious. "It was the root ball on the end of a massive tree that was washed out by the flood and drifted down the river. It was submerged just below the surface. I was relieved as the boat slid off the trunk to the right and was released from the grips of the tree. I just knew there was damage to the hull and engine and was scared shitless because it was getting dark, and as you know, I was miles from help.

"I raced into the cabin and raised the floorboard which provided me access to the bilge to validate my fears. I looked below and saw no indication of any water leakage, which brought a breath of relief. The engine was working fine, and I didn't hear any grinding or squealing sounds which indicated there was no damage to the shaft. I knew since the boat was not damaged the best option was to continue to the anchorage not far away.

"It was nearly dark when I dropped anchor and made sure the boat was steadfast. As soon as the sails were stored and the lines secured, I went below to start cooking dinner. I was anxious, and my hands were shaking slightly as I sliced the vegetables. The anxiousness was magnified as I worried about what would happen if I were to drown because you have no one else to help you.

"After dinner, I sat near the mast and admired how dark it was—the only light coming from the limitless number of stars that could be seen. To the southwest was a distant storm, and I was enjoying watching the lightning, like a fireworks show. Most of the time, the lightning streamed upward into the clouds, miles high, then there were the lightning bolts that streamed toward the ground, and I wondered what happened to the objects they hit. Then I remembered you telling me how you wished the storm in your brain would stop. That was when I looked into the heavens and prayed that your seizures would cease.

"I was exhausted and fell asleep quickly. Later in the night, a heavy downpour beat upon the deck and loudly resonated through the hull. To close the ports to prevent the rainwater from pouring in required me to jump off my berth and work fast. Lightning flashed all around the boat, but I could not hear the thunder because of the intensity of the rain. The loud sound of the rain, the consistency of the lightning, and the adrenaline rush of getting the ports closed kept me from falling back asleep. The lightning was so intense that I could see all around me without any lights and feared that the boat would be hit."

That was when Sara said, "You didn't get enough sleep, did you?"

I then told her, "My eyes were closed to allow them to rest. However, you're right. My mind never slept."

She had that expression of worry, then asked, "Did you have an aura?" She seemed relieved when I said no.

"When I sensed it was getting lighter outside, I got up and went on deck. By that time, it was very quiet and peaceful. I could see the early dawn to the east, and the boat was safe." I explained how my confidence was building as there was no indication the boat had dragged anchor, and all seemed well. "Once dressed with breakfast under my belt, I started the engine, went forward, and raised the anchor.

"I walked back to the helm and revved the engine to get underway. Having the boat underway allowed me to settle down and enjoy the ten-hour cruise to Riverside, a quaint little town along the intracoastal waterway." I smiled as I continued, "It was a hardy sail because the town was upwind and there were tides to deal with. I arrived midafternoon and found a well-kept marina to dock the boat and enjoyed walking through the area. It was wonderful to be back on shore, and I looked forward to visiting and learning about the place. Seeing the extent of the flood damage throughout the region was fascinating, and I met many people wanting to share their stories. A restaurant had reopened recently, allowing me to chill and not have to prepare my own meal."

I wanted to continue to draw a positive picture for her, so I said, "I missed you because the sunset was spectacular with all the colors of the rainbow appearing in the clouds, and I was mesmerized by an orange sky. When it got dark, I could see more stars than before and recognized several constellations. I talked to many people in the marina about which places to visit and where to anchor on future trips. It is a wonderful place, and I felt very safe and was able to sleep." After a moment, I clarified, "Although I slept lightly."

Her expression changed into a look of concern because she knew what sleep deprivation did to me. Before I could continue, another aura hit me. Sara recognized it immediately and waited quietly, watching me swallow hard and turn pale, and my speech was clearly inhibited. As it ended, she asked, "When did the auras start?"

"This morning, as the dawn came, I was awakened by that nauseous feeling that goes with it."

She had heard my stories and knew I had been through this hundreds of times before, yet even though I did not lose control of my body or mind anymore, it took me back to my darkest times. When the aura came, it affected the fear center of my brain by triggering a feeling of impending danger.

She said, "Why did you get the boat underway when you were not feeling well?"

190

"I was too far from you and needed to get home. Besides, usually, staying busy prevents the auras from occurring. I got myself engrossed in the beautiful morning sky and the quiet little town around me. You know I can use the autopilot in case of a seizure as long as there are no obstacles for many miles. Besides, after breakfast and taking my medications made me feel much better, and it seemed safe to get the sails up and continue the journey home. The wind even picked up, and the boat moved much faster. The wind was coming over the stern at that point, and it was perfect for the spinnaker." * She seemed to know the rest of the story through our experiences yet kept silent and continued to listen.

I went on, "You know how good it feels with everything rigged and under sail with the engine off, and there was a divine peace throughout the boat. I thought everything would be fine under sail and did not rely on the engine anymore. That is, until the next aura came."

She let out a sigh and asked about what happened.

"It hit me suddenly and drove fear throughout my mind and body. For control of my emotions, I slipped into my counselor mindset to do an assessment. This quieted my brain and improved my recovery by keeping the learning center of my mind busy and preventing my fear center from having control of the situation. Within a few minutes, everything seemed fine," I said, but I did not tell her how that feeling of doubt remained.

"It took four hours to reach the mouth of the river where the marina for the boat is on." I left out the part about the several auras that had occurred, each in the same manner and increasing the sensation of doubt as it enveloped the fear center of my brain. Doubt about my ability to sail, doubt about my ability to survive, and doubt about the future—all continued to grow in my mind.

---

* A spinnaker is a beautiful extra-large sail used in light winds coming from behind, which enhances the propulsion of the boat.

191

"The toughest part came where the waterway crosses the river. The ripples on the water intensified into white caps right in front of the boat. The boat was about to be blasted with a powerful wind in seconds. You know, there was little that can be done except hang onto the wheel and pray. The wind meter jumped from fifteen knots to over thirty, and I tightened my grip as the boat was slammed onto her side. The meter measuring how far the boat is healing was maxed out at forty-five degrees, and there was plenty of water coming over the rail."

She then asked, "Did the spinnaker hit the water and collapse?"

"Yes, but that was the easy part. Just as it happened, an aura in my brain went off again. I felt like I was battling storms inside and outside of my body."

She sat straight up and frantically said, "Oh my god! What did you do?"

"I hung on and waited until the boat rounded itself into the wind before I had any control to be able to steer. You would have been proud of me as I trimmed the mainsail appropriately, set the autopilot on, and then worked to bring the spinnaker down. It was snapping loudly in the wind with the sheets cracking like whips. Quite frankly, I was shocked it was not ripped in half. I quickly released the sheets and ran to the foredeck to pull the stowage sock over the top of it.[*] Of course, the sock was jammed and would not come down from the top of the mast. So, I threw all my body weight onto it, even pulling myself off the deck and nearly swinging over the side. The sock broke free, and I fell to the deck as it came down over the spinnaker, causing it to collapse as it was tucked away. I felt relieved as the loud snapping sound subsided and I had control of the boat once more."

---

[*] The sock is a giant sleeve that collapses and protects the spinnaker as the sock is pulled down over it.

I smiled and thought she would be proud of me. But she wasn't. Instead, she gave me a grave look of skepticism, then asked, "What about the aura?"

"Well, I lay on the deck, pulling the line to bring the sock all the way down." I left out the part about not wanting to stand as the aura became too intense, or how I was struggling for control of my brain.

"As soon as the aura subsided, I stood and walked to the mast, released the halyard, and lowered the spinnaker sock to the deck, tucking it away in the storage bag as it came down. I did feel a level of confusion caused by the aura, but when back in the cockpit, was able to remember which direction to steer the boat to get home." I smiled, thinking she would be impressed but, through her expression and pale face, realized she still was not.

"To increase speed, I pulled on the jib sheets, and the jib unfurled as I trimmed it properly. There came a moment of relief because the boat was once more underway, and home was less than five hours away."

Still hoping she would find some relief in what I said, I told her about the other boat that was headed to the same marina and how it brought me peace. I didn't say anything about the auras coming more frequently and my hope the people on the other boat would sense something was wrong with me if the aura spread into a full seizure. They tried to call me on the radio a number of times to check on me as they had watched what happened with the boat getting blown over. They could not get through because I forgot to turn up the volume, something that was supposed to be a standard thing to do.

I did tell her, "I won the battle because no full seizure developed."

At this point, Sara asked, "How many auras did you have?"

I had to think about this for a moment as I ran the numbers through my head—three to five per hour for over ten hours. I looked at her and said, "Somewhere between forty and fifty."

I never told her how my self-confidence was shattered by the auras or being tormented by my love for her and the war I waged again and again inside my brain. But I believed she could see this. We both knew with her condition she could have been of little support.

She looked at me with an expression of deep sadness. The darkness of my seizures had surrounded me, and she sensed my love for her being cut off. After a few minutes, she said, "I'm so sorry. I never wanted to stress you so much." With my brain racked throughout the day with the auras and fears, it took me a few minutes to comprehend her statement.

Just then, another aura struck, and the fear coming with it engulfed me in a sense of loss and despair. Once again, I realized my inability to continue to help Sara was worsened by the seizures we both suffered, and I was overwhelmed with sadness. As the aura ended, I saw Sara sitting in front of me, crying. All I could think to say was, "I'm exhausted and have to go to bed before I have another." I could no longer get close to her because I would totally break down. I have no idea when she went home.

While getting ready to get into my bed that night, I begged God, *Please bring an end to this suffering. Why is this happening, God? Why?* The times were only going to get tougher the longer I tried to care for Sara and myself. The Lord impressed upon me that my role was over. Her seizures continuing with no end in sight reminded me of when I was sinking deeper in the water and the light around me grew dimmer. When I closed my eyes this time, I felt a sense of total darkness envelop me.

Chapter 36

Sara was filled with guilt about what happened to me and decided to step away from the situation for a while. There were still a few weeks before the 90-day period would run out and maybe being away for a while would be the answer to reducing her stress and regaining control of the seizures. It was a good time for her to visit with Emily, and her epileptologist gave us advice to make sure she arrived safely. The most important part was declaring her disability with the airline so they could provide transportation at the airports and make sure she made it to any connecting flights. The airline was terrific, and this reduced her worry and stress levels, preventing any seizure-like symptoms from occurring throughout the trip. Although I missed her, it was helpful to have a couple of weeks off as her caregiver, and so my stress level could decrease dramatically.

It was in the second week of her trip when she started having minor seizures affecting her left arm and vision again. She became very concerned about this turning into a grand mal seizure and had Rick, Emily's brother, take her to the hospital. She called many times, bringing me joy when I heard her voice. Then in the second week there that joy was crushed as she said, "I'm at the hospital, and the doctors want to talk to you."

I responded, "Please give them the phone. You know I'll always try to help."

A wave of anxiety came upon me while hearing her talking to a doctor in the background and then heard his voice, "This is Dr. Snyder. Sara is having a simple seizure effecting her arm, and we understand she has been under care at a hospital with an epilepsy center. She told us you were her primary caregiver and could shed some light on her situation."

For the next fifteen minutes, I explained the history and treatment of her seizures. While I talked, I started having flashbacks of me in the emergency room with her and then in a meeting with my own doctor. I had to be careful not to confuse her symptoms and treatment with my own. Dr. Snyder thanked me for my knowledge, and the phone was given back to Sara.

"Thank you for telling the doctor what you have seen. My arm has been twitching for several days, and this morning, I started seeing double and triple again." As she said this, my worry was revived as I thought about her being alone on the long flight coming home. Once again, I expressed my concern to myself so as not to share my worry with Sara. *What happens if she has a seizure on the plane?* I thought. To get the seizures under control, Dr. Snyder recommended a higher dosage of her medication.

Her condition improved for several days, and the return trip was without incident, and she arrived back home the Sunday after she had been at the hospital. It was a joy to see her once again as we hugged each other when she came out of the airport security area. We were both ecstatic as to how well she was able to tolerate travel, and she sat in the front seat of the car with her eyes fixed upon me, holding my hand until we got back to the house. When I turned off the car, we hugged each other again, yet this time, I felt a darkness coming over us.

The storms of seizures had racked both our lives and tested our relationship. We were now sailing into the most intense storm that could destroy both of us. I now was coming over to her house to check on her every morning. On Monday morning, Sara joked with me about how many eyes I had as she was seeing six when I looked straight at her. It was troubling, especially because this lasted for several hours until she ate some breakfast. We then talked about her medication and the meager eating habits of her diet. That night, she was not feeling her normal self and went to bed early. The next morning, she had double vision, and anything she saw moving triggered a wave of nausea. She could not leave her favorite chair as this lasted into the late afternoon.

On Wednesday, she appeared better and felt good enough to go to the gym. Soon after returning home, the multi-vision problems returned. On Thursday, she woke up feeling well, but a few hours after getting out of bed, she saw double and her left arm jerked several times. I was suspicious that this was caused by a medication overdose and recommended she skip a dose. Sara did not want to stop taking her medication for fear of another seizure. I warned her if the vision issues continued, we needed to contact her neurologist.

Then Friday came. Once again, she awoke with multi-vision and hurried over to my house, where she let herself in and sat in her chair, her arm jerking and would not stop. She screamed, "Bring my emergency medication!"

I hurried into the kitchen, where we had stored some for such situations, and grabbed the pill container. In the seconds required to respond, half her body was seizing, and we struggled to get the pill under her tongue. This seizure lasted over twelve minutes, then receded as her leg quit shaking. Her arm calmed down, and her face looked almost normal again. But she still struggled with speech and the multi-vision. I saw her jubilant personality dying and hopelessness abounded because we could not understand what was happening. Her left arm would not stop jerking, and I told her, "I'm calling your neurologist."

As I described what was happening to the nurse, the seizure returned and spread from her arm back into her leg. As I watched, it distorted her entire face and spread into the rest of her body. Both sides of her brain were now affected. Her eyes would not blink as she stared off into space; her vision was gone. I went quiet as I witnessed this, and the nurse sensed something was wrong. I then told the nurse, "The seizure has relapsed and is now affecting her entire body. Sara is gone."

She responded with "Call 911. I will notify the hospital emergency room and the chief of neurology; treatment will be coordinated with Dr. Leyde. Call me back when you can."

I hung up and called 911. I briefly told them what was happening, gave them the address, and told them of the hospital's recommendation. It seemed like hours passed by as I sat and watched Sara's seizure before I heard the siren. The fire station was only five miles away, so it must have been just a few minutes. While waiting, I gently touched her forehead and calmly said, "I love you and will not leave you. You're going to be okay." Subconsciously I kept pleading under my breath, *please don't die on me now.* Within a few minutes, the ambulance pulled into the driveway, and moments later, three paramedics came running up to the house.

They asked me what had happened and then took basic information about age, relationship, etc., and how long the seizure had lasted. I told them what they needed to know as I sat with her, still gently brushing her forehead with my hand. She was given an injection of a seizure medication that freed her right side from the storm, and they moved her onto a gurney and prepared to take her out to the ambulance. I noticed one of them was very pale but kept working. As she was moved into the ambulance, I asked if I could ride along. The EMT with the pale face welcomed the idea. He would be riding with her and appreciated my presence as he felt the calmness in me. Actually, my calm demeanor was a form of shock and disbelief; I now knew what it was like for my mother when I was a child, to see me locked in a seizure.

I closed the door to the house and followed them as they carried her out to the ambulance. Suddenly, I saw myself on a gurney, being carried quickly out to an ambulance at the front of another house. I jerked my head around and saw my home which brought me out of my flashback back to the present, where I was climbing into the back of the ambulance to sit next to Sara. Part of her body continued to be locked in the seizure.

As we sped off to the hospital, I continued to tell Sara she was safe and loved. I knew she could hear me now because half her mouth smiled. The EMT wiped the blood off her face that came from her chewing her tongue and lip. That was when he asked me, "How many times have you seen this happen?"

All I could say was, "Several."

"How do you know what to do?"

"I have lived with my own seizures for many years, and now I am being the caregiver of someone who has them too. I have also been a mentor helping people and families that live with epilepsy."

"So that explains why you are so calm about this."

I gave him a very serious look and said, "I may appear calm, but on the inside, I am as pale as you. Unlike all the other people I've helped, now I'm caring for someone I love, and it is ripping me apart. I'll collapse when she is safe. I just can't do that right now because you all need me."

He looked straight at me and put his hand on my shoulder and said, "God has put you in the right place. Your apparent calmness sure has helped us." It was a reminder of how God had been with me many times before; even so, a tear formed and streamed down my face. I didn't bother to wipe it away.

When Sara was brought into the emergency room, the staff was waiting and took her into an exam room for evaluation. The seizure appeared to have nearly stopped, and Sara was exhausted. In the meantime, I held my composure and called Jennifer to tell her what happened. Fortunately, she could walk with a cane and drive again. She immediately came to the hospital to be with me. I stayed beside Sara, holding her right hand and assuring her she would get through all this and be whole again.

I did not see my sister approaching as my back was turned toward the entrance to the room. She put her hand on my shoulder, and upon seeing her, I buried my head in her shoulder and broke down, sobbing. She held me tightly and didn't say a word as she was looking right at Sara. That was when Sara covered her eyes with her right hand, and her half smile vanished as she saw what her seizures were doing to me, half of her cried too.

It would be another hour before the seizure was brought totally under control, and Sara was admitted to the hospital for several days. Once she was in bed and safe, I kissed her goodbye and reassured her of my coming back to be with her. Jennifer's driving home brought some relief because not only was this experience emotionally difficult, but it triggered a couple of intense auras too. To maintain some level of control of my emotions and auras, the counselor in me tried to take over my thoughts by attempting to process what had actually happened. I was not doing very well in that. The pastoral part finally came through and reminded me to "Trust in the Lord. All things are possible."

On the drive back, I told Jennifer how the home I once cherished now seemed like a bloodied battlefield, with blood on the floor and couch. When we arrived in the house, Jennifer offered to stay with me, afraid I would relapse with my own seizures or despair. I declined, then as I walked through the front door, I wished I hadn't. Sara's chair was right in front of me. The chair reminded me of the Sara I cared so much about yet could no longer provide care for. I was physically and mentally spent but beyond sleep. Seeing the empty chair worsened my sadness and canceled out my ability follow what I had been taught and practiced as a counselor. My mind raced into the past through flashbacks of Sara and her seizures.

I lost a close friend again. Just before I moved to the Eastern Shore my best friend, whom I considered my brother, died in a car accident when he had a seizure. Now the person whom God had brought to me was ripped from my arms and engulfed in the disease that I had combatted throughout my life. I wept and could no longer stay in the place I worked so hard to make my home. With tears streaming down my face, I ran out to my car and drove to Jennifer's home. Seeing my car in the driveway she knew what had happened and she flew out of her house and hugged me, taking me back to reality. Here was a safe place, and within a few minutes, my exhaustion overcame the adrenaline that was pumped up by the events which took place over the past several days and months. I slept for several hours, but exhaustion still enveloped me when I woke up.

Visiting Sara was confusing. When I entered her hospital, I was brought back to the Johns Hopkins Epilepsy Center every time. Terrified by my flashbacks and the thought that I may lose the person whom I loved and who loved me, my past fears of dying from a seizure seemed to be coming true, except I had imagined my own death, not Sara's. The auras with the anxiety attacks, nausea, and flashbacks now began from the time I saw the hospital Sara was in till I drove away later in the day. It would take several minutes after visiting with her and talking to the doctors before I regained the confidence I needed to drive home. The fear of seizures was overwhelming me—both hers and mine. It was my love for her that gave me the strength to overcome the fears, but the horror was intensely overwhelming and was taking its toll.

Sara was there for three days, and the neurologists were like me. They could not determine if the symptoms were initiated by the seizure medication or caused by a seizure breaking through the protection of the medication. It took another week of Trish and I monitoring her at home before the test came back, and it was determined the medication had reached a very toxic level for her body—so toxic that it was actually triggering the seizures.

At home, I kept thinking about ways I could care for Sara and realized the love I had for her. She was no longer the person I had known because she was struggling like me. I needed to take some time off and someone else had to take on the responsibility of caring for her. Would a peace come within me when she was with someone else, or would this person rely on me and would my obligation return? The only way I could survive this was to follow the role of a counselor who had control of any and all emotional feelings and to be the caregiver who took care of her daily needs, burying my soul in order to protect my brain from the onslaught of the seizures.

This time, the doctors recommended reducing the dosage of her current medication, and we waited for the blood level to reach the point that the drugs were beneficial and not a detriment to her health. The medication Dr. Leyde was cautious about was prescribed, and Sara still had her emergency pill. The new medication made her tired and impaired her ability to function. I was getting more distraught as Sara faded away into the doldrums of drugs. This time, the new medication was working, yet it took several more days before Sara was functional again. However, I was terrified and remained in the caregiver survival mode.

Suddenly the sense of relief came back to me in the present day as I found myself back in the auditorium. I was holding tightly onto the edge of the podium and my fingers ached. I was overcome by a sense of sadness and could not say anything for a few minutes. I then noticed how the people in the audience were quiet, yet many were having difficulty sitting still in their seats; there was a sense of uneasiness in the room. I began to wonder, *Was this caused by a relationship those in the audience may have had with a close friend or family member whose health was declining?* or *Was it due to something they see in me?* The counselor part of me was engaged as I observed what was happening. I controlled my emotions and my grip loosened, it was time to continue.

Chapter 37

The end of the period of getting Sara's seizures under control had come. When it started it seemed her seizures were close to being totally under control, but as the end of the three months approached, they came more often with greater intensity. It was obvious the trigger was the fear of losing what she always dreamed of and for a few months seemed almost possible. Sometimes, the seizure would only affect her arm and leg, but now they spread throughout her body, leaving us isolated in the living room with her in the reclining chair.

It had been a year and a half since I'd met Sara, yet it seemed we had known each other for most of our lives; we had so much in common and could relate with each other that well. There were times there seemed to be a future in our friendship and a huge potential for us to work with each other. It seemed we were destined to help others find hope and a belief in God, but now we struggled trying to find hope, especially Sara. Control of her seizures had not come soon enough to allow our concerns and fears to diminish. I hoped for and looked forward to seeing Sara back working full-time in her church again, but we had run out of time.

The stress of losing her job and her dreams being crushed triggered her inability to eat and sleep, along with increasing blood pressure and anxiety. All these issues were also key triggers to her seizures. Trish was a tremendous help; however, she had developed a fear of Sara's seizures as they left her nearly powerless. There were a few times she called me in the night, just knowing Sara was about to have a seizure but then the seizure would never develop. Multiple calls were coming daily, making me relive my past, except this time it was not a memory; all this was happening all over again. I started to have auras several times a week, and the uncertainty of whether a seizure was coming was hitting me hard, inside and out.

We no longer talked about the future. It was a difficult subject, but she needed to be prepared for the worse case too. Chris and some other member of the Church Board were to come at 7:00 PM that night.

She finally gathered the courage to ask, "What did you do when this happened?"

She was referring to my work as a project manager. I told her, "I had been defeated by the seizures, then broken by the surgery. It was very hard to write the letter I did to my boss to tell him about my inability to function as a manager and that I needed help. It tore me apart, and I felt defeated, but I never gave up hope. It was possible to have hope as my manager believed in me. I think the church counsel believes in you too. You are already a miracle in your survival from the stroke, even more with your recovery. Now you must survive the seizures and the stress. You just need some time off to identify your disabilities and triggers, then turn them into abilities like I did. Just never stop believing in yourself.

"You need to exercise your brain and make the impossible possible once again. Try doing some of the things I did. Sudoku is a good start to working with numbers and recognizing patterns. You'll start to get better. You may never be in charge of a church again, but you are always going to be a pastor. Think about all the other parts of the church where you can be of service, you'll be able to deliver a powerful message even if it isn't from a pulpit."

She looked straight at me, with tears streaming down her face. I reached over and hugged her as she let herself cry. I did not know which was worse: watching her seizures or holding this broken woman as she wept. I held her tight and kept silent.

It seemed to be forever until she gently pushed herself away and looked at me. She whispered, "I'm so sorry," as she saw my shirt soaked with her tears.

I cracked a half smile and said, "It will dry out and, just like you, everything will get better. It took me ten years to recover. It should not take you as long because you have someone who cares for you and wants to work with you. Be like me. You must believe. The good Lord introduced me to a new line of work through my experience. Maybe you will be the pastor who works with people requiring a special calling. God will never give up on you. Just trust in Him."

She looked down and said, "I need some time alone now. I'm going back to my study to pray." A period of isolation that would never end had begun for Sara.

Upon closing the door to her house, thoughts of my own recovery came back to my mind. A rush of anxiety hit, and it felt like an aura was about to start. Knowing Sara's condition and my inability to help made me hurry away. I was away from her home and the changed setting allowed the anxiety to fade away.

We did not have dinner together, as I didn't have much of an appetite, and she was not able to eat anything. Chris and his staff were on time and we sat in the living room, and it seemed like the executioner had arrived, and Chris was not playing the role well, as he was pretty choked up and had some difficulty speaking. That was when another member of the board spoke up, "Pastor Sara, you have been fired and have three days to vacate your office. The church will pay for one more month of rental on this house, then it is your responsibility. Your condition is unacceptable and cannot be tolerated in the church. Is this clear?"

Sara looked as if she had been slapped, Chris and several other members were in shock as they stared at their cohort, and I was enraged. Before I could explode, I stood up, walked over to the fellow and quietly, but firmly said, "Follow me." He looked perturbed but seeing the expression on my face, complied immediately. Once in the front yard I turned sharply around and looked straight into his eyes and said, "Your message is received. You're the type who like to inflict scathing pain, using the Bible to make you the judge and jury of the disabled. You're the one with the lost soul. Leave!" I doubt he even heard what I said, as he was looking down at my hands that I had unknowingly clenched. When he heard me say, "leave," he ran to his car.

I returned to the house to find Craig and the others comforting Sara, and everyone was offering to help and provide her a place to stay if necessary. The whole time she never said a word, just sat there staring at her hands. Craig, on his way out, told me she could stay as long as necessary. I thanked him and let him know that I would be a source of help and would be in touch. It was a very solemn night.

My memory faded and I found myself on stage once again. My hands were clenched again, and deep feelings of frustration were fading into a darkness that enshrouded me again. Carol saw me looking down and came over. She had the lights turned up, and I barely heard her say "Be sure to be back tomorrow, Thursday, at ten o'clock so you can hear Mr. Johnson's evaluation of his experience and we may have time for some questions." She then smiled at me and once again said, "Call me early tomorrow if you will not be able to make it. I will understand."

Something made me stand up straight, as I thanked her for the opportunity. Looking up, I saw a pastor who had not moved from his seat and kept his eyes upon me as everyone else was leaving. I did not wait to meet him because I had a stronger urge to meet with someone else down the hall. I wasn't sure who, but I knew they were waiting for me.

Chapter 38

While walking down the hallway, several people approached me and started asking for a few minutes of my time. I could not remember all their names, but every one of them had a family member or close friend struggling with seizures or a stroke. They reminded me that we were never alone in such situations and this aided in my recovery knowing that many people struggle with the battle I'd been fully engaged in. Several talked of the fear of losing a loved one who they could not leave. After several minutes, I asked if anyone knew of a room we could go to with some chairs we could use as I was awfully tired of standing. They all got excited that I was willing to spend some time with them and not just leave. There was a lounge not far away, and I truly appreciated the ability to sit which was a godsend.

Linda told me of her seventeen-year-old daughter who struggled with partial seizures, which occurred often at school when taking an exam. Dianne was scared of her husband, who would suddenly jump out of bed and run down the hallway and out into the yard. Gary was worried about his one-year-old son, who started having complex seizures several times a day a few weeks earlier. Alex asked about my ability to get through school after having brain surgery. There were several other people wanting to learn more about epilepsy and how they should approach clients and family members. Audrey and Malcolm wanted to know more about stroke recovery because of their experience with a parent.

The stress in their faces diminished as each person told more of their story. Linda appreciated the resources everyone was able to provide as information to the teachers, on how to respond to her daughter's seizures, along with some of the causes to consider that could be triggers to them happening. Dianne appreciated the feedback from several other people about how to keep her husband from running out of the house during his seizure and the importance of having neighbors she can call on at any time for help. Gary's situation was the most difficult as young children with seizures can die from suffocation. We talked of resources online, monitoring systems, and finding a child epileptologist to see. By the time he had left, several people had found doctors, and one even scheduled an appointment for him.

Telling Alex more about my experience getting through graduate school brought another flashback. This time, it was good for me. It was a memory of being together with Jessica, sharing how we both struggled with seizures and brain surgery. My getting through the courses in graduate school inspired her to complete the program too. I could not help but smile for a moment.

Audrey's mother had a stroke two months earlier and was still partially paralyzed and with a slur in her speech. Malcolm's father had one a few weeks earlier and was in a rehabilitation center. They both talked of how their parents had given up hope of recovery. I offered what I learned through my experience with Sara and the research that helped with my recovery from surgery. The most important parts of my talk were the desire and drive to recover through a faith that God was working through you. Repeating things over and over and keeping motivated should be expected, especially after the temptation to quit arises.

Without thinking, I told them, "With God, all things are possible." The moment I said this, I felt a warm feeling come over me as Audrey smiled and thanked me for the information. She said, "Mom and I have always been faithful. You have provided real examples to use to emphasize the importance of never quitting."

Malcolm thanked me as well, then wanted to know more because his father, who was in his sixties, never talked of having faith. I looked at him and said, "Seems like it is time to ask him about it. Then tell him he has an opportunity to set an example for others if he lets God work through him. He must work hard to want to recover with no expectations except what God conveys. You'll be surprised by what you'll see. Just remember, like me, it will take years of work through faith."

No one realized how much time had gone by, and it seemed everyone was late for something. I asked each of them what they were learning as they heard my story, then had everyone share and listen to one another's stories. Several said they were hopeful, knowing that they were not alone in the struggle they faced along with their new contacts. Everyone wanted to shake my hand, and many gave me a hug as they said a word of thanks and expressed how much they looked forward to hearing my talk the next day. They did not realize how they inspired the courage I needed to get through the next day, the toughest day of the presentation.

My mission was clearly not over. In fact, the meeting indicated the start of a new beginning for me. I felt a warm feeling within me.

Section V

Recovery

It was Friday morning and still dark outside. I slept rather well and felt safe, like everything was as it should be. Then I remembered why I was in a hotel room, and fear took hold. I started to pray and asked for the strength it would take to carry me through the day. The memory of the evening before came back and filled me with courage, the courage I needed to overcome my fears. The encouragement came through the meeting of the day before with the people dealing with the trauma of epilepsy and strokes in their lives and the lives of their loved ones. They now became the support I needed to win the mental battle going on within me. I got out of bed and got myself prepared to face the past and the battle from within.

The conflict was still ongoing when Carol introduced me. I was apprehensive of my ability to talk about such a horrendous moment in my life and this fed the fears. I knew giving the talk was part of my recovery and gave reason to stand behind the podium, to relive those events one more time, something I had already done in therapy. I had in my hand a copy of the speech presented at the conference on epilepsy the week that Sara had left her house. It provided a summary of everything that happened with Sara as part of the closure to this seminar. I was looking at it as the house lights dimmed, then waited for the words to come to my mind that would lead up to presenting the speech to this group.

For several minutes, there was complete silence. I stared at the paper to keep my fears in check, and I gathered the thoughts I needed to explain what happened. Then it was time to look up from the document in my hand and let the words flow.

Chapter 39

It took several days after my sailing trip for my brain to recover enough to get ready for the conference I was to participate in, and everything that had happened with Sara was very taxing on my mind. There was a speech I needed to prepare and research to do that required much of my time. Sara realized what an important program this was and how much it meant to me. After dinner that night, she asked if I had some time to talk about our future. Knowing how important this was for both of us, I didn't want to wait and dropped everything I was doing. We walked to the living room where we could sit close to each other.

She began with "I appreciate how much you have helped me, but I am holding you back in your work and my seizures have stressed you out. You have been incredibly kind and devoted to me, but I have seen what it is doing to you and I can't stay here." Tears started running down her cheeks as she continued, "I am not getting better, and everything I thought would come together for us will never happen. The only reason I'm still here is that I have fallen in love with you. You have cared so much for me with a devotion I have never witnessed before. My inability to serve the Lord and the stress my seizures are causing you will eventually trigger your own complex seizures again. To prevent this, I'll be moving to California and be close to Emily."

I felt devastated, yet no tears came; maybe I had temporarily fallen into a survival mode which tempered my emotions. "You have seen what's happened to me and that I'm not capable to continue with the responsibility of being your caregiver. I know you need to leave, Sara, but I want to stay in touch with you. I want us to continue to be a part of each other's life. We need to be able to see each other occasionally."

Just as I said this an emotional blast suddenly came from my past. I was sitting on a couch by myself, absorbed in defeat by my own seizures. At that time, the seizures had control of my brain, just like now. This time, the trigger for this seizure came through my soul, squeezed by my love for Sara. Her suffering tore into my emotions as they had never done in the past. That was when we looked at each other with tears streaming down our faces, feeling defeated and at a total loss.

To regain control, she got up and walked away, leaving the front door open as she ran to her house. Nearly an hour passed before I gathered the strength to get up and close the door. My support system through prayer seemed closed off, and only the walls could hear me.

The more we discussed her moving, the better things seemed to become, as I would no longer have to be her full-time caregiver anymore, yet we could stay in close contact. She had been in contact with some of Emily's friends who were thrilled that they could help with her recovery. She was comfortable with the arrangements that were made and was excited we could continue to stay in touch and see each other on occasion.

A lot had to happen before Sara could move, and it would not be completed in time before I had to leave for the conference. Sara made arrangements to visit with Emily for several weeks and to work with Emily's friends on finding her a home in that area. She would return for a short while to finish getting her things ready for the move and the church provided her a few extra weeks to make it easier. To reduce her stress and the fear of seizures, we talked of my coming to visit and doing some sightseeing on the west coast, then fly back together.

Separating from one another for a while would give me some time to recover as someone else familiar with her condition would have full responsibility. I was actually looking forward to being apart from her for nearly a month as I needed a break. Even though she was a close friend, taking it upon myself to carry many of her life burdens was something counselors were never supposed to do. But Sara was not my client and letting go of her as she suffered seemed opposite of what I should have done.

Chapter 40

As I was busy preparing for the epilepsy conference, Sara was able to start organizing all her personal possessions for moving. I took it as a positive sign that she was improving, for such organizing was difficult for anyone. Her workouts at the gym made her capable of handling it physically. Her mental capacity was improving with her new medication and control of her seizures. I cheered her on not only to encourage her, but also because I saw a vast improvement in her abilities. She could not achieve this work even just a month ago. She said she was proud of herself but never really smiled, and something else was missing.

As I saw some improvement with her mental abilities, I thought we finally had the right mix of medications to control her seizures. The medication seemed to be having minimal impact on her capabilities. Maybe the Sara I had fallen in love with months earlier was returning. I tried not to get my hopes up because she had relapsed several other times in the past.

Her personality gradually changed since she was placed on the new medication. Initially, everything seemed all right. We were both filled with hope as the seizures were brought under control. Even her arm stopped jerking. We actually talked of working together in a year or so based on how well her recovery was going. I was so overjoyed about not fearing that she would have seizures anymore that I was not neglected to notice the other changes in her. In fact, I was slightly troubled when a few days before I left for the board meeting, she seemed to lack emotion when she talked. She neither smiled nor frowned. Not once did she mention love for anyone or any desire to be with other friends and family, like she had done so many times in the past. She simply stated facts in almost a cold tone of voice.

It was a couple of days before I left when Trish called and asked if I could help Sara to apply for disability insurance. "You need to come see what's happening," she said. When I arrived, Sara was on the phone trying to explain to a social worker what had happened over the past year and kept mixing everything up. She set the phone down when she saw me drawing out a timeline of events for her. After she studied it for a while, she looked at me and said, "I have no memory of any of this happening." Then she said, "I have no memory of what happened since moving to this town"—referring to the same time frame of when her seizures had started. She looked right at me, and the twinkle in her eyes was gone, replaced by an expression of defeat. Now I knew why Dr. Leyde would not prescribe this medication to Sara, because she knew how it would alter her character.

I was shocked and devastated but hid it. If she had no memory, she was no longer aware of the care and love I had for her or the mental stress her seizures had on me all that time. I was crushed, but I managed to subdue my emotions by going home and absorbing myself in the work I needed to complete prior to the conference. On my walk home, I prayed once more by silently crying out, *God please, please! Don't let the Sara I knew die on me!*

For the next two days, I focused on my work and did not hear from Sara. Then it was time for me to drive the six hours to a friend's house where I would spend the night before going over to the hotel where the conference was being held the next day. I went over to Sara's to give her a hug and told her that I still loved her. She did not say anything or hug me back but gave a simple smile as I walked out the door.

I held my emotions within me until going around the side of her house to say goodbye to Samuel, who ran up to me with a ball in his mouth. When he realized I was not there to play, he dropped his ball and gave me a very sad look. A premonition came upon me that this would be the last time I would ever see him. Tears began to flow down my face as I rubbed his chin, so I quickly headed to my car and drove away. I wiped my tears away and concentrated on driving down the road to regain control of my emotions. As I increased the distance between me and Sara, the control became easier.

Chapter 41

I hadn't seen my friend for several years, and we had much to catch up on. He was amazed by my story about Sara and hoped everything would come together for us. We went to church that evening where many of the congregation recognized me and wanted to hear about my journey. A peace came over me while being among the people whom I had known for many years and had provided the care I needed to recover from surgery. They provided this care again that evening, not realizing they were providing me a safe haven from the storms of stress.

The next day, I arrived at the hotel where the conference was taking place. There were many people at the opening session, and we each shared our backgrounds. There were to be several speakers that night to share their experiences in living with disabilities. I was the first to speak about the needs of those struggling with seizures. I began with my background of living with seizures, the necessity of brain surgery, and the struggle to recover—the toughest part of which were the unknowns of seizures and the stigmas they carry.

The main part of my presentation focused on the caregivers—be they the parents, the children, or a friend. I talked of how caregivers struggle as much as the person with epilepsy as they witness a seizure, the degeneration of that person's personality and abilities, and the side effects of medications that can be as traumatic as the seizures themselves. The most difficult part I had to present was my role of being a caregiver.

Suddenly I couldn't talk and looked up from the podium, trying to see who was in front of me. Carol was looking right at me, like she was about to get up. I then realized what needed to be done, and I looked at the speech in my hand. Once more, I had to suppress the feeling of sadness before continuing. Tears had formed but had not fallen over the edge of my eyes as had happened prior. My training as a counselor reminded me, *You must calm down. Take a deep breath, and release it slowly. The control will come, and all you have to do is read the words.* Upon releasing my breath, I automatically took another and then started to read.

"Last year, I had a new neighbor who had a stroke several months earlier, and the doctors did not believe she would survive. She came to speak with me because she kept seeing the same thing over and over again, even though it happened only once; and her eyes were continuously moving. The intensity of her seizures slowly progressed to where she was having complex seizures several times a week, and I became her primary caregiver. Her seizures lasted for many hours. I know the importance of staying calm and positive in such times, but this was very difficult because I had flashbacks of my own experiences. Throughout the seizures, she could hear my voice, and it brought her a sense of peace when I arrived to take care of her.

"She had little memory of what happened last year. Only recently had a new medication been applied, and we had seen the seizures brought under control. For a moment, I was able to associate with a piece of the person I originally met. Although the seizures were controlled; that person was gone. The outlook was not looking good.

They say epilepsy affects one in twenty-seven people. If we considered the mental stress on the caregivers, the number of people affected increases three to fivefold; even those who witness a seizure often struggle with some level of post-traumatic stress disorder. We need to make sure the recommendations for first aid include not only the person with epilepsy but also those who witness the seizures. Programs need to be established for the mental health of the caregivers."

This time, the setting felt different than when I gave the speech at the conference, and I felt an urge to do something different. I looked around and said, "This time, let us have a moment of silence to pray for the disabled and their caregivers."

Many heads bowed as the silence fell. During this moment, I had to fight back the tears as memories of Sara flashed through my mind, held in check by a room filled with prayer.

Now for the toughest part. *Deep breath, slow release, now.*

Chapter 42

Sara departed to be with Emily and Rick, Emily's husband, the day I had left for the conference. Arrangements had been made for Samuel to go with her. While I was relieved because I was no longer her caregiver, I missed her as a friend. The day I got home from the conference, Emily texted me that Sara had forgotten to pack her medications, along with many clothing basics. They needed to know the dosage and have the medications shipped immediately. I knew the urgency, so I quickly gathered the prescriptions from her house and took them to the post office to mail them overnight.

We stayed in touch initially nearly every day via text messages, but after the second week, I rarely heard from her. She responded to my inquiries with the basic "yes" and "no" answers. She always talked about not having any seizures or symptoms since the last time being in the hospital, over two months ago. It seemed like we could be together again because they were controlled for the longest time since my meeting her. The time for my visit was coming up fast, so I spent a Sunday morning comparing airfare. She was to call me when it was time for me to come. I barely realized that not once in her text or phone calls did she mention the word *love*, like she normally did. Nor had I heard her laugh on the phone like she so often had in the past. I should have realized something was happening when she stopped answering my texts or returning my calls for several days. Being optimistic, I guessed it was an issue with her cell phone.

It was early on a Monday morning and I was headed out the door to help a friend do some home repairs when my cell phone rang. I was excited to answer it because Sara's name was announced, and her phone number displayed. She must be calling to plan my trip to visit with her.

Instead, it was Rick, whose voice seemed sad as he said, "I wanted to tell you Sara will not be coming back your way to get her furniture. Something has happened, and it is best she just stays with us."

When I heard this, I froze in my tracks and my mouth fell agape. I nearly dropped my tool bag and the phone as I replied, "I thought she was getting better." I felt like someone kicked me in the gut and I couldn't breathe. I had hung on to the hope that she would get better. Now came the time where I had to face the reality of the situation.

He paused, waiting for me to say more, but I was in a state of shock. He then continued with "I'd noticed since she got here that she seldom laughed. Sometimes her voice would go flat. She told me she couldn't recall what happened before today, like her memory was gone. When I asked her what town she lived in, she couldn't tell me. Then I asked her if she knew you, and she gave me a confused look and asked me to repeat the name. This all came to a climax about a week ago. I didn't want to tell you then because I did not know if her memory would come back or not. We took her to the hospital and, after a series of test, were told she may have had a mild stroke. Due to the condition of her brain from the previous stroke, they couldn't confirm that anything new had actually happened."

I was in a daze as I listened. My hopes were crushed, and I could not respond. It was surreal and I did not want to accept what I just heard, even though there were many indicators in the past that this was bound to happen. Any thoughts of Sara fully recovering had just dissipated in my mind. As this was all crashing down inside of me, an aura hit but this time a calm voice from within me said, "Hold yourself together." I then collected myself and managed to rattle out, "I'm in shock. She seemed to be doing so much better." The words then got jumbled in my head but after a moment I was able to add, "I need some time to think about what you just said. Give me a day or two, and I'll be in touch."

Rick understood. "I'm sorry to have to tell you this. I know this must be tough, but please call me back soon," he said. I hung up and sat down, the aura continued for a couple of minutes then the confusion it caused in my brain was calmed along with my emotions and it subsided and went away.

I just didn't want to believe what was happening, and I still wanted to cling to the hope that somehow another miracle would occur, and Sara would return. I was in a state of shock as I sat in the chair and stared at the floor. What was tearing me apart was the reality that Sara was not going to get better. All I could think of now was how she was isolated from me both physically and mentally. All I could say to myself was, "This must have been some kind of bad joke. How could this be happening after how we had come together, our common interests, and spiritual beliefs? This was just not real. My god, she was a good person. How could this be happening?"

I tried to make a list of the key events in our lives, but I could not write any words. I was struggling to control my emotions, and my organizational skills were still awry. It had been obvious to me that Sara's mental abilities had been declining but I had refused to accept it. I felt my faith was broken as I struggled to understand what had happened. I thought, *Why and how could we lose to epilepsy when it was such a miracle that Sara recovered from the stroke? It seemed that I was in the right place to help Sara, and many people thought our relationship was through a divine intervention. If it was, why has our relationship been crushed so cruelly?*

My soul was bleeding. I stayed at Jennifer's house that night and never closed my eyes. The next day, I returned to my house to start packing Sara's possessions. While walking in the door, I was overcome with grief as I realized that she was gone. The strokes and seizures were causing more damage to her brain, wiping out the possibility of her ever recovering to the person I once was developing a deep relationship with.

I had been taught that one manner of handling grief was to remove everything that would remind a client of the person they lost. I wanted to get her furniture out of my house; but it was too large to move, and professionals were required. It could not even be hidden because it was in the living room near the front door. Every time I walked in and saw it, despair would overcome me. In fact, it hurt to be anywhere in the house, and it felt worse than dealing with someone who died because death at least signifies the end of their life. A strong feeling overcame me that even *hope*, which was at the center of my survival, was a farce.

I had taken on Sara's struggle with seizures which drew me into a relationship that would nearly kill me. The situation was very real, and all hope was lost and overcome with grief. It would not take long before I lost control of my mental self and I was buried in hopelessness. The flood gates of despair were now fully open, and I was dashed down the river of loss into the hands of grief.

The despair led to me relive the storms of the seizures that overwhelmed both of us. My faith had been challenged before, yet I felt God was always with me. This was the second time I lost a very close friend to seizures. We believed our coming together was God's way of helping both of us heal. But the loss went much deeper this time and convinced me that God had no plan in the agony we were living, and that our coming together was just a happenstance. For a moment there, I swore vehemently that there was no God.

Suddenly, I began to relive the past fifty years of my life, the times I was broken by seizures and struggling with the unknowns of surgery and recovery. Epilepsy had cost me a piece of my childhood, threatened my carrier, destroyed my family, damaged my memory, and rocked my faith and abilities. Now it tore a hole through my heart and drove a knife deep into my soul. The emotional part of my brain then became the focal point, and for nearly an hour, I broke down and sobbed and could not stop. Everything that I had been dealt with as someone with epilepsy crashed against the caregiver in me. Suicidal ideations now traversed my brain, which was driven by thoughts of being an absolute failure. At that moment, there was no God, only pain—the more intense pain of watching a loved one going through an even deeper hell than I had endured. I could not stay in that house any longer, and I moved out within a few days.

The most difficult part was that no one knew of my work, sacrifice, or love for Sara, not even Sara herself, who has no memory of me. The only solace that I could receive would come from God, but at that moment, I was blinded from Him by my past and emotions. I was a broken man.

For a moment, I once again felt nothing. I was oblivious to standing in the open in front of a large group of people. The difference this time was that I had no feelings of anger, sadness, despair, or grief—only emptiness. It was like I was standing in a vacuum with no sound or light. I closed my eyes and listened to my breathing; I inhaled slowly, held my breath for a moment, and then exhaled. While starting my next breath, I opened my eyes and could see the audience in front of me.

Everything was real again. I was okay. It was now time to move on.

Chapter 43

It had been two days since Rick's phone call when I had the stamina to start making arrangements with a moving company. My desire to remember the Sara who knew me, made me laugh, and cared for me, ate away at me. I never wanted to lose her and struggled for nearly a year as a friend, mentor, and caregiver to bring her back. At one point, she was to get better, and we could eventually work together through our ministries. But realizing she was now gone and would never return wiped away any of the good memories and left me with remembering a person struggling with seizures. If I were to heal, I needed her possessions moved out of my house. I found a respectful moving company in the area and called Rick to finalize the arrangements. I wondered if I was going to feel sad or happy when the movers came to take away Sara's property.

As my house was emptied of her furniture, I felt a sense of both relief and despair. Relief, because I made sure everything was packed properly and taken away from both homes. As I walked through the house and no longer saw anything that reminded me of her finalized the fact that she was gone. I felt defeated, that I lost the battle and guilt that I had misled her.

I had taken down the sign over my hallway door which said "With God, all things are possible" because God had cut me off from the person I cared so much for. I tossed it into the trash can because to me, God did not exist then. After the moving van drove away, I heard a voice say, "Good job, Matt!" I wondered if it was God that was talking to me. It took a moment for me to realize what I heard and went back outside to retrieve the sign. *If all things were possible through, God, then why did all this happen?*

The house seemed empty with just my possessions left in it. The living room echoed the sound of my steps as I walked across the hardwood floor. The emptiness of the room magnified my loss. Sadness enveloped me.

I struggled with sleepless nights, searching for an answer to what happened. The question of "Why was I able to recover from brain injury but Sara declined after doing so well?" kept repeating in my mind, with no answer in sight. A week later, my seizures returned, triggered by the exhaustion and grief. Anxiety overcame me as the nauseous waves of auras struck several times an hour, driving home the hopelessness I felt. I was tortured as they were a reminder of why Sara was gone. I even wished to experience the more intense seizures I used to have because they would wipe out my memory for days. The numerous auras were embedding into my soul from the loss of Sara.

Rick was very helpful as he made sure he had Sara eventually call me. It would not be until she was settled into a nursing home when I received a call from her. I was taking a nap when my phone rang and announced her name. I woke up and answered it.

She started the conversation by saying, "Thank you for making sure all my furniture and possessions were moved. Rick said you did most of the work, and he kept telling me to call and thank you."

My desire to cry out to her was kept in check as I realized that everything that happened was for the best. I responded with "You're welcome. Do you remember ever living near me?"

"Oh yes. Samuel liked your backyard and visiting your nice house. My seizures are under control now. I haven't had one for a long time."

I then asked her, "What type of boat did we go out on?" There was a silence. I then asked, "Am I taller or shorter than you?"

She replied, "You are definitely taller than me, and I liked to put my head on your shoulder."

227

I then told her, "It was nice to hear from you. I hope everything goes well. Goodbye."

Before I could hit the end call button, Sara responded, "Matt, I have little memory, but am trying to find it again. I struggle doing the first level of the Sudoku but will never quit trying. I can't recall your name when asked, but hearing it brings me a calm feeling and a sense of peace envelops me. I just wish I could remember why." There was a moment of silence, then she said, "Goodbye."

As I hung up the phone, I realized Rick was correct about her condition. She could give no definitive answer about the boat, and in actuality I was shorter than her. I shed no tears this time. I lost her to the stroke and seizures, but I knew the woman I'd worked so hard to bring recovery to still loved me the best she could.

It would be weeks of controlling my emotions before I could fully understand that Sara's decision to leave was based on her love for me. She knew how much I cared for her and realized the pain her condition was causing me along with the decline of her mental abilities. What I wish she knew was that losing her was far greater than any kind of trauma I endured throughout my life. I had watched her be sucked into the hell I had endured in my past and then I lost her completely.

People who knew Sara through her role as a pastor would ask me how she was doing. When I was asked what happened, I would tell them of her symptoms getting worse and that no recovery was expected. I had a harder time, however, to answer when asked, "How are you doing?" without my eyes welling up in tears. I still felt in my emotional state at that moment, that God had abandoned us.

Chapter 44

My emotions took control again and if I continued to talk about what happened to Sara, I would be swept up in them as I had been before. It was time to talk about PTSD and how it applied to my situation. I approached the subject from the perspective of a counselor to keep myself together. Another deep breath and a sip of water, and it was time to continue.

Eventually, I read about people who suffer from hemorrhagic strokes and learned the average life expectancy is less than five years. I had known Sara during the end of the first year and the beginning of the second and realized was I blessed with not having to watch her physically die one day. She demonstrated a love for me when she was able to realize what was happening to both of us and thought it best to leave. She was more a realist than I and knew her condition was only going to get worse, and if recovery were to ever happen, it would take many years. Samuel was the only one she could continue to love because she was not a burden to him.

Sara's seizures had brought back the terror of my past. Losing her was the spark that ignited the dread in me to explode. It would take several days for me to regain some control in order to start working on understanding what truly happened. Through my work as a counselor, I was aware that events like the loss of Sara could be a trigger to something larger. A fundamental technique was for me to write down everything I imagined which fed my despair. The first step in my recovery required several weeks of me sitting on a couch with a computer on my lap.

As I typed, there were times I would be filled with anger, and I would bang on the keys of the computer. Other times, my vision would be blurred by tears, and I would struggle to see what I had written. I remembered the despair of my future being threatened, nearly injuring my children and the death of my best friend who had a seizure while driving. The overwhelming fear I had was worsened with the thought of death as I felt a seizure coming and not being able to stop it. Would I be able to recover, or would this be the one that would take my life? During the first few days, I had to be reminded to eat and I slept on the couch as I lost track of time.

The mental damage was intensified by my repeated near-death experiences. The body may not die during a seizure; however, the person may. Picture it like a thunderstorm bearing down on you. The preictal stage is seeing the dark clouds approaching and the flashes of lightning, then hearing the rumbles of thunder, and smelling the ozone. Knowing what such a storm can do brings on feelings of trepidation, or even dread, in those who have experienced it. The ictal stage is comparable to when the lightning strikes, overwhelming some area in the mind. Some or all the brain is then lost in the ensuing electrical storm it is enveloped in, like wires overloaded and burning in a building. Various senses may turn on and off in an attempt to bring awareness of what is happening and can further establish the hopelessness of the situation. The postictal stage is the recovery from the storm. There is damage left and the brain must reset, and the parts need to rewire to enable one to regain control. Then the storm strikes again, and this process reoccurs once or many times. The distress of the storm returning becomes a constant. Those who witness the impact of such storms, especially the love ones, are hit just as hard.

The indicators of PTSD may seem small at first, then they begin to escalate as more seizures are witnessed. Having people available who can help with the trauma that was experienced is what they need. Unfortunately, in the part of the country where this story occurred, there were no support organizations for people with epilepsy. The hospitals were not capable of providing the needed mental health support nor were there any counselors available who could comprehend the situation and were able to provide more support aside from empathy.

Writing helped me organize all the events that led to my breakdown and to realize the mass trauma I had lived through. It began with my first seizure as a young child, and then how the medication affected my personality and mental abilities. Then the return of the seizures and the impact this had on my classmates and friends. There was fear instilled in my children and wife by my brain surgery, and the years of recovery. I wrote many entries about how a foreboding happened nearly every day, fed by the trauma of having a seizure, of rejection by friends and family, of losing my job and career, of possibly dying.

This led to my discovery that over the years, the distresses of my seizures were buried one at a time in my mind. What happened with Sara brought these all together and then crammed them into my memory in one massive blow. The culmination of the events intensified the injury to my self-esteem. Writing it out was like peeling an onion. I was pulling the layers off in tracks of time and events. The situation with Sara was the spark that caused the explosion of emotions that disabled my ability to think rationally. I was knocked to the ground, unable to get up this time. It was similar to battling a massive seizure, which had control of me, like a giant hurricane, that goes on for days. What saved me was my training as a counselor and applying hands-on what I had been taught.

After I wrote everything down, the turmoil in my mind lessened, and I was able to apply myself to other tasks. It was like having a heavy burden lifted from my shoulders but left me physically and mentally exhausted.

The battle had grown in intensity and then had to be fought on two fronts. Dealing with Sara's seizures had slowly awakened an angry giant within me—a giant that had to be dealt with, and the earlier the better. The battle with the giant in me had to be won first, before facing her seizures. Reminders about Sara filled me with depression. My hope was crushed, and it seemed that fighting my own giant, now fully awake, was not worth the effort. I was living with PTSD, leaving me with the question, would I be left as a broken or stronger man? The answer has been slow in coming.

Reading back through it all amazed me with how much I had endured over the years. More of the reality of the story became known with every reading. It was like watching a very sad movie where the first time left you crying, just a tear formed the second time you watched, and after that, just feelings of sadness. For me, there were still several unanswered questions all starting with the word *why*. *Why did we come together? Why couldn't she get better and be a minister? Why did God allow this?*

There were several people who helped carry me through while I struggled through this. Some were friends who kept me busy and took me out of my storm zone, which was the neighborhood with the houses and the towns with the places the seizures occurred. There were the strangers I had helped over the past year who thanked me for my time and efforts. Some believe the Lord brought them back to my life because I needed their smiles and appreciation, like a reminder of the other good things I had accomplished and to remember how God was always looking after us.

Another part of the healing process was my going back to my house and finishing the renovations. I kept seeing Sara in her chair having seizures in the living room and her pounding on the window on the porch to get my attention as she slipped away again into the hell of the unknown. The flashbacks never included any of the good times we had. They were all memories of her being in the house when she was having a seizure—be it the simple with only her arm jerking, or the complex, with her losing consciousness and me timing the ictal stage.

It was very difficult to hold back tears at first, but the more I stayed at the house, the easier it became. I could not stop, however, the sense of failure. Once I completed the renovation work, the house was placed on the market for sale. The memories I had there were focused on the seizures, both Sara's and my own, and it was no longer a healthy place for me to be in. Being there made me think about ways to get Sara to come back, but I knew her immediate recovery was impossible. Once the house was sold, I realized that the person I thought would be a large part of my life and I would work together with in service to the community was forever gone.

Chapter 45

I had done well in controlling myself. Now it was time to finish. I reminded myself, *Just summarize everything; don't drift off into any dreams.*

Throughout my life, I fought with seizures and nearly lost the battle several times. All the other battles were within my brain. This time, I was like a soldier who had recovered physically, only to watch a close colleague die from a similar wound. This form of injury was the most difficult because it cut through my heart, leaving scars deeply embedded in my soul.

I wished I could just be with the Sara who would go to dinner with me and walk along the waterfront, who would show me how to cook and made me laugh as she danced in the kitchen and made funny faces, the Sara who came up behind me and pulled on my shoulders to make me stand straight to feel proud of myself and my accomplishments and to not be ashamed by my health and seizures. The same Sara who hugged me several times a day and surrounded me with a love I had never before experienced. She was the person who motivated me to sail even bigger boats and venture out on the water where God surrounded you.

I still have dreams that Sara will one day be able to sail to the cape with me and see the wonders of nature and the life on the sea, where the water is clear and the sky is magnificent—the clouds are God's artwork filled with magnificent colors as they are decorated with the rays of the sun as it rises and sets; to listen to the ocean waves and feel the softness of the breeze, to enjoy the evenings where the storms are many miles away and provided the most magnificent fireworks of the heavens with their lightning as they tried to outdo one another. If only these storms had occurred externally and not in our brains.

I snapped back to the present, barely aware of the auditorium. My eyes felt full of tears, and I was staring at the floor. There was no more to say. I just stood there, feeling totally alone. Then I heard someone clapping their hands, then another, and another. Suddenly, the whole room was filled with the sound of applause. I looked up and saw everyone standing and clapping. They reminded me of what I had learned listening to such stories other people shared, and I also benefited through their experience. I looked up and felt whole once more.

The pastor whom I noticed the day before waited as several people wanted to talk to me. He was still seated and was the last person left, even after Carol. He saw how tired I was and invited me to sit next to him instead of walking up to me. He introduced himself as Luke and told me about his background as a pastor. It turned out we had gone to the same college, where he learned about me going through the program. He was interested in hearing about my story because he had knowledge of epilepsy from experience with a close friend's child.

He spoke, "You're still missing something, and I know someone who can help. His name is John, and I work for him at a church downtown. He said he knows you when I told him about this conference and what you had talked about. He would like to meet with you. Are you available at nine o'clock tomorrow?" He then added with a grin, "He said he owes you."

John and I had much in common. He was the pastor of a church I had attended, and we had been through the same pastoral counseling program. We had helped each other through our common experiences, and he had me deliver the sermon a few times. We kept in touch with each other about once a year and he knew of my meeting Sara, but not the outcome. I breathed a sigh of relief, then chuckled, knowing I owed John more than I could ever repay.

"Please let him know that I really appreciate his offer and will be there tomorrow," I responded.

"Great. I'll update him on what you talked about today. That was quite an experience you've had. I really appreciate you sharing how your faith was tested and were still able to come through. We'll be praying for you and Sara. It was a pleasure meeting you."

Chapter 46

John greeted me at the front door of his church the next morning with a huge smile and a firm handshake. "Welcome, Matt. I heard you've been on quite a journey with Sara and wondered if I could help." I followed him to his office where we had met for many years when he was my pastor and mentor. John had shared much about his life as we worked together and related well with me through his own experiences with epilepsy. He set an example by never wavering from what he believed in and always going straight to the problem at hand.

After getting seated and briefly talking about my sailing and his fishing on the bay, he said, "Luke told me what happened to Sara. When we last talked you told me about meeting her and the bright prospects of working together. I am sorry it turned out the way it did. I'd like to help, especially because of how the sermon you gave several years ago about the importance of hope in dire times helped me tremendously when my son was stricken with seizures."

"My experience is similar to yours, John, except unlike your son, her seizures got progressively worse, and the medications wiped out her personality," I replied.

He gave a half smile. "Matt, what I tell you, you probably already know through your experience and studies. It takes at least a year to recover from the loss of someone close. In time, you may become more focused on the positive. Your case is more complicated because the loss is associated with places and situations that took you back in time. You relived some troubling events that occurred way before you met Sara."

I looked up at him. "You're right. There are places that trigger vivid memories of Sara's and my own seizures. I cannot even go near the church she worked in. Taking care of her totally burned me out mentally, emotionally, and physically. I have worked on eliminating the reminders yet cannot get rid of them all. Being near the water in the early mornings or evenings is the toughest. While looking at the heavens, I still wonder, *Why do such things happen?*"

John looked at me with his inquisitive eyes, like he was reading my mind. "That is what you need to explore within yourself, Matt."

I felt a little uncomfortable but continued with, "I try to stay busy to keep myself from dwelling on the loss, but I cannot get her off my mind. I find with each passing day the dreams I create fade away. When new ones come along, I dwell on them for a while, then the reality of the past sets in, and they melt away too."

John asked, "What was so special about your relationship?"

"We started as friends, then mentors for each other, and were excited about working together in a ministry someday. Our experiences and pastoral work seemed to match up in being able to help throughout the community. Not only that, my experience gave her hope as it seemed to be what she needed to fully recover."

He kept his eyes locked on mine. "When did you accept the reality of the situation?"

I thought for a moment. "At the start, her seizures were sporadic and simple, and I had little problem helping her. Then they progressed, coming more often with greater intensity. We were not prepared with a backup plan, and were fighting from both sides, our present and my past. The only way to control her seizures was through a medication that wiped out her personality."

John was aware of the medication's side effects because his son had been on them too. His response followed suit. "Then the person you cared so much for was gone?"

I knew the answer but just didn't want to accept it. "That's what happened. There were times she seemed to improve but was actually getting worse. Based on my own experience, I knew her abilities were declining as the seizures continued. You're right. I was watching her slowly slip away but had faith she would recover," I said.

The seriousness of his expression meant that the counselor in him was coming out. "How much of what you were dealing with was associated with your caring for Sara and how much was from the trauma you lived with prior to meeting her?"

I contemplated what he asked. Then I said, "Her seizures were the trigger that set off my horrific memories. Flashbacks occurred every time we went to a hospital. As her seizures intensified, they took me back into the days when I was traumatized by my own. The terror of the unknown was reawakened and nearly blew me away."

John's analysis came: "You have lived with the traumas your seizures caused for many years and did a remarkable job of surviving and through faith never gave up hope. The traumas you lived with were chronic, reoccurring. You were engulfed by the present and the past, from within and around you. It was the perfect storm, that overwhelmed you. Your ability to talk to a group about what happened is a good indication you have control of the PTSD now. It may never go away but it should no longer inundate you. Flashbacks may happen, but you have developed a manner to maintain control." He paused, then said, "Something else still has a hold of you."

I looked down at the floor and quietly said, "I survived, but she didn't. I failed her."

He responded, "You're thinking like an engineer and rationalizing everything. You used the word *failed* but have not addressed what that's based on."

I scornfully replied, "I led Sara to believe she would get better, but it did not happen. I let her down." I looked at my trembling hands, feeling like I had let go of a person needing to be rescued, then watched as they drowned.

He waited, knowing that I needed time to face what had just been brought to the surface—guilt. A silence followed as I looked up at him, searching for forgiveness. He could read it in my face and said, "Let go of the guilt you created through the role you believed you were to fulfill. The magnitude of what you're dealing with is beyond what anyone could have endured. You could not change the outcome, Matt."

Anger raged through me. "But I thought God had a role in our coming together, that we were going to be working with each other!"

He looked away for a moment, waiting to say the words that I should have already known. His calm voice pulled the anger out of the room. "Matt, I believe your caring for her was God's intention and what kept her alive and working in her ministry. Both of you initially had the same experience of caring and expressing a love for other people. You demonstrated how far that love could go in your relationship. Even though it was based on a short time with each other, you demonstrated unconditional love. You cared for her even more because of her disability.

"Your feelings of failure and guilt need to be replaced with joy, the type of joy that comes from living through a difficult time yet still having faith in God, which makes you stronger in the end. Appreciation comes through trial, Matt. Just remember, the outcome of her health could not be avoided. She is in the good hands of several caring and loving people who can also support one another. Her decision to leave, when she still had some reasoning skills, was in everyone's best interest."

He could tell I needed time to absorb what he said, and patiently waited. Eventually I said, "I'm realizing that it was the trauma we suffered with that made our friendship stronger." I then asked the question I had been seeking an answer to for a long time. "Where was God in the times when Sara's seizures became so intense?"

Applying his own experience, John replied, "The Lord put both of you in a position to take care of each other. He provided hope through your sharing of what it was like to live with the unknowns of seizures. She probably would not have been able to continue her ministry for so long, have gotten the appropriate medical care, or ever gone sailing like she did without knowing that the Lord was with both of you."

As his words sank in, I sat up straighter. "But why couldn't she get better?"

"I'm not sure. The type of ministry the two of you were planning was not what God planned. God's plans are bigger than we can comprehend. We only get to see a small part sometimes. But people in need are God's tools in helping us understand the importance of giving and caring for others. The caregivers often receive more joy because they witness how precious life really is. The work they do is a ministry in itself. However, the prolonged stress that must be endured in some situations can lead to burnout, and the ability to comprehend what is really happening is lost. Time away from such situations is what is needed to recover. That's why I'm away from the church for a few weeks a year.

"In order to learn more about yourself your mind needs time to calm down, before processing the experience. Just having a day or two doesn't allow enough time for the mental stress to subside and comprehend how to better handle those tough situations."

I was beginning to have a clearer understanding of how this applied to myself. Even though Sara was away from me a few times, the stress of her condition was always with me. It reached the point where my brain was exhausted and caused my seizures to return. "So that's why there's a team of people caring for her now in the nursing home. They can support one another and not have to carry as high a level of responsibility for too long," John said.

He continued, "Matt, your experience is a reminder of how precious life really is. Every day is special. You can read about a terrible event but cannot comprehend the magnitude of it unless you've actually lived it. Even though it was shaken, your faith has been the key to your survival. There is a time and purpose to everything."

"If only I could understand the purpose," I replied.

He then said, "I remember the emotional burnout I experienced with my son and the feeling of being a burden to those who came to help. God was actually working through them, enabling me to recover and become a stronger person through faith. My son's ability to live with his disability and the people who helped us led to my changing careers and becoming a pastor. I was a caregiver in need of support and they were God's tool as they came to the rescue, providing all kinds of support, even if just through prayer. It was all a lesson about God's grace. Now answer this question: Where did the support for you and Sara come from while you were going through all this?"

In some ways, this was easy because I had already answered this in my presentation earlier this week. "My sister, the church members, then the EMS, the doctors and medical staff, the construction workers, and Trish, to name a few. Even Samuel the dog. Support came through their faith and experiences. Prayer came through many, including the church members, but I never heard the answer because it was not what I expected."

Now, everything we had been talking about came together for me and I quietly acknowledged, "My role was not to see Sara recover as I expected." I paused for a moment while remembering her telling me how my voice brought her a feeling of safety and calmness to her while she was in the midst of a seizure. "My role was to help her overcome the fright caused by the seizures, to provide a sense of peace while she endured the storm occurring from within.

"I witnessed how such an experience helps others through a group I met with recently. There was a role in my sharing my experiences that provided hope to others in what may seem to be a hopeless situation. Now the people in the group have one another when facing their life storms."

John smiled. "Matt, you have lived with the trauma of epilepsy for many years. You were never allowed to face the reality of it, because of the fear of rejection, forcing you to bury your emotions in order to survive. Sara's condition uncovered what you had hidden inside and made you face it. Take some time to process it all. Working with these groups is a clear indication that what you lived through has made you stronger and this will further your abilities in applying yourself in the tough situations that may come along. Like with me, this experience will strengthen you in your ministry, preparing you for the future."

Suddenly, there was a presence in the room that could not be described. Everything seemed brighter and the air was easier to breathe. The pain and sorrow were washed away, and, like John, I was sitting fully straight once more, filled with a peace I had not felt in over a year, and I smiled without needing to force it. He must have seen the relief that came upon me because he continued, "Thank you for sharing. You allowed me to be a witness to God's grace again. May many people recover from their experiences through the hope stories like yours instill in them. Just continue to learn how God works through each and every one of us."

He smiled broadly as he concluded, "Finish washing away any feelings of guilt hanging on you and find more ways to apply yourself. Go exploring on your boat before you go back to work. I hope during the next time we meet, we can talk about your adventures."

The burden I had dragged into his office was lifted. It was time for me to leave. I felt stronger and even taller as we stood up. "Thank you for helping me face what was dragging me down. The sadness is still with me, but the guilt is replaced with the joy in realizing we were never alone in what we went through. You have been a tremendous help in allowing me to release the memories of the good times we had. It's time for me to go home and plan a sailing adventure. I'm looking forward to talking to you someday about my experiences that have less trauma and happier endings."

John said, "Amen!"

Epilogue

Understanding Post-Traumatic Stress Disorder and Epilepsy

Suffering produces endurance, and endurance produces character,
and character produces hope.
—Romans 5:3–4, Revised Standard
Version of the Bible

Post-traumatic stress disorder, or PTSD, comes from the trauma a person has lived through or witnessed, which results in flashbacks of the event or events, creating feelings of deep sadness to high levels of anxiety or depression. Flashbacks may be triggered by hearing sounds or seeing an object that was present during such events. Severe depression may set in, and suicide may be considered or can be attempted in extreme cases. Most people eventually pull out of the shock they experience. They tuck it away in a file in their brain and move on.

PTSD was not officially recognized for veterans until after the Vietnam War. Although post-traumatic stress has been identified for centuries based on the experiences of combat personnel and known as shell shock, battle fatigue, or Vietnam syndrome, little has been researched and quantified in the civilian sector. Some of the most heavily impacted by PTSD are those who witnessed the same trauma over and over again—like those working in the medical field, in emergency response, or others who have lived through traumatic experiences themselves, which have left them emotionally and mentally scarred. Alcoholism and drug abuse seemed to be a manner of self-treatment. It was not until 1980 that the criteria for diagnosis of PTSD was added to the American Psychiatric Association (APA) to its Diagnostic and Statistical Manual of Mental Disorders (DSM-III) to be applied by those in the mental health fields.

Trying to explain to people what it is like living with epilepsy is difficult unless the person has experienced a seizure. There is what can be seen, such as the physical injury, and the unseen, which is the battle going on within the brain, that leaves emotional and mental damage behind. The name for the three stages of a seizure are based on the word *ictal* (a Latin word that means "a sudden attack of a disease, mostly affiliated with strokes or seizures"). The preictal stage is an odd feeling or premonition that provides a person a moment to prepare before losing consciousness. For others, there is no preictal stage, and no warning that a seizure is coming. They lose consciousness, which often results in physical injury from falling and their not being able to protect themselves. Concussions can occur, and in some cases, this happens so often that the concussions become continuous.

There are many levels to the ictal stage. The ones presented in this story were the most difficult for the person suffering from epilepsy as they were aware of what was happening. Seizures that occur without any awareness at this stage are easier to endure. The fear of dying or not coming out of a seizure whole is shut off. The ability to watch what was happening or to hear voices during this stage keeps the sufferer in a reality: the reality of having no control. A child who suffers from a seizure who hears his parents scream or can watch people react as they run away from or laugh at them leaves a heavy feeling of despair and helplessness.

The postictal or recovery stage is when the person struggles with the emotional impact of what has happened. This may be amplified because it is part of a seizure or living with the reality of "being different." Anger, depression, defeat, brokenness, fear, anxiety, and dread are natural feelings, often due to how other people react or the result of the seizure and the damage it has caused to the brain. The struggle to remember names, the processing of information that once could be done in less than a second, or the inability to identify people or locations leads to a sense of defeat that feeds an ongoing anxiety. The caregiver may become emotionally torn apart, wondering if the person they love will ever return, fears driven by ignorance or poor information about the situation.

Seizures are typically dramatic for all involved. What adds to the situation for those having the seizure is when they are able to see or hear how other people react. If only seizures were much simpler and easier to comprehend or were a disability that can be seen on a constant basis. The best way to handle it is with communication. The issue is the seizures, not the person who has them.

Having studied PTSD, I know that its treatment is based on cognitive behavioral therapy (CBT). This involves challenging negative patterns of thoughts or unhelpful cognitive distortions that lead to depression and anxiety. Attempting to deal with a series of repetitive traumas leads to distortion by magnifying the fear of the events, leaving a person overwhelmed. The technique I applied to bring myself back to reality was to write about what had happened at nearly every instance an event upset me or left a troubled memory. I had a lot of emotional pain to endure as the memories of the wounds they inflicted were relived, often blurred by tears of the memories of defeat and the anger of loss. To get through this, I kept telling myself, "Just give it three months." I had no idea what would happen then but knew it would take time for life to get better. And it did.

A significant part of the recovery came when I reviewed what I had written and as I remembered the experiences involved in helping others who were struggling with chronic illnesses. As my emotions settled, I remembered that my role as a mentor and counselor was not to cure them of the illness. It was to help them find a sense of peace while they lived through what they had to endure. I was amazed as I realized the vast number of pages I had written and read how many times death seemed so close. I realized how God was always with me and this brought a sense of peace and renewed in me a hope for a future. I saw how many times recovery occurred, and it made me realize that survival was not a matter of luck, that the Lord was indeed with me through those around me.

Only a small portion of the actual events have been included in this story. I hope that those of you who are living with trauma in your lives can learn how writing and talking about what you have experienced can bring about some level of recovery. For those of you struggling from a stroke and/or epilepsy, just never give up—being a person in need makes you God's tool in helping others fulfill a calling for them to practice being good people through their support and love for you.

I believe there is a God with a master plan for each of us. To try and determine the eventual outcome for everyone is impossible, but God has given each of us an ability to endure. It requires patience and a belief during times of trial that things will get better. Often, what we receive is greater than what is hoped for. Overall, we become stronger with time and knowledge as the character of who we are is built. I pray that you can endure the times that test the limits of your abilities and that they leave you as a greater, more compassionate, and hopeful person.

More information about living seizures and epilepsy may be found in the book *Weathering the Storms: Living with and Understanding Epilepsy*. It includes some of the history and medical information about seizures and what I have lived with—including my brain surgery, which required years of recovery—and my work as a counselor and friend to people struggling with the trauma of epilepsy.

Appendixes

Appendix A
Basic Guide for Caregivers

1. Don't panic! It shuts down your brain's ability to reason and respond appropriately.
2. Be aware that the individual in need may be able to see and/or hear what is happening.
3. Protect the head with a cushion, pillow, or soft object; your hands work well too.
4. Talk to the person throughout the stages of their seizure or stroke in a calm voice to reflect you care and are with them. Use simple statements such as "You're safe. I am with you."
5. Set up a support system, especially if you cannot lift the person. This can be a neighbor or a close friend.
6. Keep a list of the medications, including dosage and time of day they are administered. Have a copy available to give to emergency personnel and those providing medical assistance or treatment.
7. Find people you can talk to about what you are experiencing. You may find groups near you or on Facebook. You may also contact your local chapter of the *Epilepsy Foundation* to obtain training and other information.
8. Be sure to take care of yourself. Take time to do what you like to do, especially in relieving stress.
9. Seek help through family or friends. You can only be a good caregiver if you are healthy.
10. Obtain professional counseling to help manage the stress of being a caregiver.
11. Seek emergency support when the following occur:

Seizures

a. If the seizure last five minutes longer (ictal state) than usual or the person has difficulty breathing

b. If the person has recurring seizures in a short period of time

c. If the seizure causes injury to the body or head

You need the support to handle the situation. When you have any doubts about the outcome, call 911. Remember, they will respond to provide emergency treatment and transport if they and you deem it necessary.

Be prepared to give first aid to those who may have witnessed the individual having a seizure. This involves sharing information.

Strokes[*]

Call 911 immediately when you or someone else has any of the following symptoms. Act FAST.

F—Face: If one side droops when asked to smile

A—Arms: Ask the person to raise both, and one droops down.

S—Speech: Ask them to repeat a simple phrase if their speech is slurred or they cannot say it.

T—Time: Time is of the essence. The longer this happens, the more damage to the brain will occur. Call 911 without question.

---

[*] Information found through the Center of Disease Control (CDC) and other agencies

Appendix B
Seizure Stages and the Senses

Seizure Stages

There are three stages to a seizure: preictal, ictal, and postictal. The preictal stage is when a person is cognitive of what is around them, yet they have an odd feeling, taste, premonition, déjà vu, or sudden motion with a hand or foot.

The ictal stage occurs as the seizure continues to spread over part or all of the brain. At first, the person becomes quiet, motionless, and stares straight ahead. Then depending on how far the seizure spreads, the body may stiffen and shake as the muscles tighten, sometimes to a point where they are injured by tearing. Breathing may stop temporarily. Some people are not able to hold their urine and may vomit, chew, grind their teeth, or clap their hands. This phase is most difficult to watch and often leave memories imprinted in the caregiver's mind.

The postictal stage begins when the brain resets and the person is able to regain control. This may last for a few minutes or take days to fully recover. When I had seizures that started in my left temporal lobe, my ability to speak would take several minutes to a few hours to return, and it could take several days for me to fully assemble thoughts. Since my surgery, total recovery took only a few hours.

Seizures and the Senses

A person's five senses and their responsiveness are affected by where a seizure begins. Some people have seizures that start in the occipital lobe, and their vision is impaired. If the nerves continue to become overly excited, the seizure spreads to other sections of the brain and affects their other senses and abilities. If seizures begin in the hippocampus, the memory is affected. Often, the seizure spreads to the adjacent areas, impacting vision, speech, and hearing. The centers of speech and memory recover slowly, and although the person can talk, their ability to comprehend and remember takes more time to fully recover. They may be more fearful of what is happening around them, or they may no longer laugh and play. Their inability to recall or recognize words may interfere with speech and reading skills.

Appendix C
Types of Seizures

Some types of seizures include the following:[*]

Generalized seizures. Generalized seizures involve both sides of the brain. There is a loss of consciousness, and a postictal state after the seizure occurs. Types of generalized seizures include the following:

> *Absence seizures* (also called petit mal seizures). These seizures are characterized by a brief, altered state of consciousness and staring episodes. Typically, the person's posture is maintained during the seizure. The mouth or face may twitch, or the eyes may blink rapidly. The seizure usually lasts no longer than thirty seconds. When the seizure is over, the person may not recall what just occurred and may go on with his or her activities, acting as though nothing happened. These seizures may occur several times a day. This type of seizure is sometimes mistaken for a learning problem or behavioral problem. Absence seizures almost always start between the ages of four to twelve years.[†]

> *Generalized tonic-clonic seizures* (GTC, or also called grand mal seizures). The classic form of this kind of

---

[*] From the Johns Hopkins Medicine Health Library under nervous system disorders, epilepsy, and seizures

[†] Absence—the earlier childhood absences almost always remit by late childhood; the later childhood ones (e.g., age of onset: six to eight) are called juvenile absences and usually continue and form tonic-clonic seizures in adulthood.

seizure, which may not occur in every case, is characterized by five distinct phases. The body, arms, and legs will flex (contract), extend (straighten out), and tremor (shake), followed by a clonic period (contraction and relaxation of the muscles) and the postictal period. Not all these phases may be seen in everyone with this type of seizure. During the postictal period, the person may be sleepy, have problems with vision or speech, and may have a bad headache, fatigue, or body aches. [*]

Myoclonic seizures. This type of seizure refers to quick movements or sudden jerking of a group of muscles. These seizures tend to occur in clusters, meaning they may occur several times a day or for several days in a row.

Focal or partial seizures. Focal seizures take place when abnormal electrical brain function occurs in one or more areas of one side of the brain. Focal seizures may also be called partial seizures. With focal seizures, particularly with complex focal seizures, a person may experience an aura or premonition before the seizure occurs. The most common aura involves feelings such as déjà vu, impending doom, fear, or euphoria. Visual changes, hearing abnormalities, or changes in the sense of smell can also be auras. Two types of focal seizures include the following:

---

[*] The bilateral tonic-clonic seizures are, by far, the most dangerous. They often cause brief postictal paralysis with impaired breathing. Those who have seizures out of sleep while facedown are at special risk for asphyxiation (SUDEP).

255

Simple focal seizures. The person may have different symptoms depending on which area of the brain is involved. If the abnormal electrical brain function is in the occipital lobe (the back part of the brain that is involved with vision), sight may be altered, but muscles are more commonly affected. The seizure activity is limited to an isolated muscle group, such as the fingers, or to larger muscles in the arms and legs. Consciousness is not lost in this type of seizure. The person may also experience sweating and nausea or may become pale.

Complex focal seizures. This type of seizure commonly occurs in the temporal lobe of the brain—the area of the brain that controls emotion and memory function. Consciousness is usually lost during these seizures. Losing consciousness may not always mean that a person passes out; sometimes, a person stops being aware of what's going on around him or her. The person may look awake but may have a variety of unusual behaviors. These behaviors may range from gagging, lip smacking, running, screaming, crying, or laughing. When the person regains consciousness, he or she may complain of being tired or sleepy after the seizure. This is called the postictal period.

Appendix D
Seizure Classification

When diagnosed with epilepsy in 1964, there were only two types of seizures at that time: petit mal and grand mal. Through medical research, according to the Epilepsy Foundation of America, seizures have now been identified and categorized into three major groups:[*]

1. *Generalized onset seizures* affect both sides of the brain or groups of cells on both sides of the brain at the same time. This term was used before and still includes seizure types like *tonic-clonic*, *absence*, or *atonic*, to name a few. There are two categories of symptoms:
   - Motor symptoms may include sustained rhythmical jerking movements (*clonic*), muscles becoming weak or limp (*atonic*), muscles becoming tense or rigid (*tonic*), brief muscle twitching (*myoclonus*), or epileptic spasms (body flexes and extends repeatedly).
   - Nonmotor symptoms are usually called *absence seizures*. These can be typical or *atypical absence seizures* (staring spells). Absence seizures can also have brief twitches (*myoclonus*) that can

[*] The Epilepsy Foundation of America and Epilepsy Foundation are federally registered trademarks of the Epilepsy Foundation of America Inc. The information is from their website: https://www.epilepsy.com/learn/types-seizures.

affect a specific part of the body or just the eyelids.

2. *Focal onset seizure* has replaced the category of *partial seizures* because the term *focal* is more accurate when talking about where seizures begin. Focal seizures can start in one area or group of cells in one side of the brain. Focal onset seizures are categorized based on the person's level of awareness during the seizure. This includes the following:

- *Focal onset aware seizures* occur when a person is awake and aware during a seizure. This used to be called a simple partial seizure. Motor symptoms may include jerking (*clonic*), muscles becoming limp or weak (*atonic*), tense or rigid muscles (*tonic*), brief muscle twitching (*myoclonus*), or epileptic spasms. There may also be automatisms or repeated automatic movements, like clapping or rubbing of hands, lip smacking or chewing, or running.

- *Focal onset impaired awareness seizures* occur when a person is confused or their awareness is affected in some way during a focal seizure. This used to be called a complex partial seizure.

3. *Unknown onset seizures.* When the beginning of a seizure is not known, it's called an unknown onset seizure. A seizure could also be called an unknown onset if it's not witnessed or seen by anyone. An example is when a seizure happens at night or when a person lives alone. As more information is learned, an unknown onset seizure may later be diagnosed as a focal or generalized seizure.

More about the Author

When I was nineteen years old, I struggled with depression caused by being diagnosed with epilepsy for the second time and from the side effects of medication. The problems were amplified for me and my family by the traumas of the past. Seeing the word *HOPE* on the Rhode Island state seal, where I was studying at a university to obtain a degree in Civil Engineering, brought meaning to what was happening to me, and, at the time, made me a stronger person. It was the simple concept of hope that helped me to focus on my future, which led to my graduating from my class, doing well with my career, and having a family. In fact, epilepsy became just a part of my past until the seizures started to break through the protection provided by medication, eventually becoming intractable, or untreatable. The dark days had returned. The stress caused by the fear of having a seizure became the trigger that started them. Surgery to have a section of my brain removed became the only option. Hope became a large part of my recovery, leading to my becoming a mentor through the American Epilepsy Foundation HOPE program. HOPE was the acronym for Helping Other People with Epilepsy.

Through my own experience with epilepsy, after having been diagnosed at the age of four, I have witnessed others being afraid of me and I was discriminated against. Once in a while, an area of my brain would create an electrical storm, causing other areas to become inundated and lose control. Often, during a seizure, I could see what was happening around me but could not respond as I watched my children explain to the paramedics what was wrong with their dad.

As a mentor and counselor, I helped many people who have witnessed a person have a grand mal seizure and listened as they expressed their fear and the trauma they endured. They often felt they should have done more. Eventually, all my knowledge about epilepsy would not be enough to help achieve what I hoped for several people. Their condition progressively got worse and I severely underestimated the role of the caregiver, even though I applied my personal experience and what I had learned through my studies. I felt broken.

Soon after working through a major phase of recovery, I helped a father give first aid to his young daughter who was having a grand mal seizure. I was able to effectively help both. The tears flowed when the little girl, who could not speak, gave me a long hug as her way to thank me. She'll never understand how the Lord worked through her that day. Her disability and love helped me realize that everything that had happened to me made me stronger and more empathetic to those struggling with similar trauma. It was a lesson on how God works through everyone who suffers—the person with the condition and those who love and care for them.

Find out more at:

www.jonsadlerbooks.com

www.ingramcontent.com/pod-product-compliance
Lightning Source LLC
Chambersburg PA
CBHW060232050426
42448CB00009B/1406